KEYSTONES for READING

COMPREHENSION ▪ VOCABULARY ▪ STUDY SKILLS

Level C

Alden J. Moe, Ph.D.
Louisiana State University

Sandra S. Dahl, Ph.D.
University of Wisconsin

Carol J. Hopkins, Ph.D.
Purdue University

John W. Miller, Ph.D.
Georgia Southern College

Elayne Ackerman Moe, M.Ed.
Louisiana State Department of Education

MODERN CURRICULUM PRESS
Cleveland ▪ Toronto

Table of Contents

A Kind of Richness

What does it mean to be rich? If you have a great deal of money, you might say you were rich. If you have a happy life, you are rich in another way. In this lesson, you will read about a man who found richness living in the wilderness. You will learn some special words.

1 KEYS to Content Words

Special stories need special words.

LEARN Some stories have a special vocabulary.

DIRECTIONS Read the content words and their meanings. They will help you understand the paragraph below.

A. pioneer: one who is the first to do something
B. settler: one who goes to live where no one lived before
C. wilderness: a natural place with no settlers

In 1769 Daniel Boone left civilization to explore the Kentucky wilderness. There were no settlers in Kentucky. Daniel Boone and his helpers had to cut the Wilderness Road through the vast land. In the next five years, 200,000 settlers followed the road made by this great pioneer.

DIRECTIONS Write the correct word to complete each sentence.

1. Daniel Boone was a _____ who explored Kentucky.

2. Many _____ followed him.

3. Before the road was made, Kentucky was a _____.

② Practice With Content Words

DIRECTIONS Study the vocabulary words. Write the letter of the correct word on the line in each sentence.

A. explore: to travel to an unknown place to learn more about it

B. mineral spring: water, rich in natural elements, which flows from the ground

C. ridge: a range of hills

D. roam: travel with no special route in mind

E. salt lick: a place for animals to lick up salt in the earth

F. settlement: a place where people built their homes, especially in a frontier area

G. skeleton: the bony framework of an animal's body

H. stretch: a large, unbroken area of land

1. Daniel saw a _____ of land between him and the river.

2. Wild animals used to _____ through the wilderness.

3. Deer come to the _____ to drink every day.

4. Boonesborough was the first _____ in Kentucky.

5. From the top of the _____, you can see miles of forest.

6. Daniel Boone was the first to _____ the Kentucky wilderness.

7. He made a knife from a bone of a deer's _____.

8. The trampled ground showed that many animals came to the _____.

DIRECTIONS Read more about Daniel Boone. Use what you read to help you answer the questions on the next page.

Daniel Boone returned to the wilderness many times. He roamed through magnificent forests that took his breath away. Every kind of tree he had ever seen seemed to be growing there. He saw ash trees that he guessed must be fifty feet high.

Daniel found salt licks where mineral springs gushed from the ground. Wild animals coming to lick the salty ground had trampled out a wide path. Beside one of the salt licks, he found the bones of a gigantic creature. He picked up a tooth which must have weighed five pounds. Then, using one of the skeleton's huge bones for a stool, he sat down and ate his evening meal.

Later Daniel stood on a ridge and gazed over a great stretch of land. He felt like the king of the universe. It was a wild, free feeling that almost swept him off his feet. He felt rich. He was glad he had had the chance to explore the countryside.

One of Daniel Boone's explorations into the wilderness lasted for three months. He felt that he would never be the same again. He had grown to know himself. He had discovered what was important and what had no lasting value. More than ever, the feeling grew within him that his life had a purpose. He had work to do. That work was to lead his family and other men, women, and children into the wilderness to build a settlement in the new land called Kentucky.

Answer the questions below.

1. What word in the story means a natural place with no settlers?

   _____

2. Which word in the story means to wander with no special plan in mind?

   _____

3. What word in the story tells us that the forests were beautiful?

   _____

4. Why did wild animals come to the salt lick? _____

   _____

5. Who had already made a path in the wilderness? _____

   _____

6. What did Daniel use for a stool? _____

7. What does stretch mean in this story? _____

   _____

8. Why did Daniel feel rich? _____

   _____

9. Which word in the story means to travel to an unknown place to learn

   more about it? _____

10. What did Daniel decide was his purpose in life? _____

    _____

11. Which word in the story means a place on the frontier where people

    built new homes? _____

Different subjects have their own vocabulary.

4 Content Words

Words About Cities

When you read about life on a farm, you find words like *pasture, livestock,* and *tractor.* When you read about city life, you read words like *citizen, population,* and *commercial.* In this lesson, you will learn the definitions of these and other words as you read about life in a city.

 1 KEYS to Words About Cities

Special words tell about cities.

LEARN We use many special words to talk about cities. They tell us about the government, the people, and the business of cities.

DIRECTIONS Read the definitions of the words about cities. Complete the paragraph by writing the correct word on each line.

A. residential: refers to the part of the city where people live
B. citizens: people who live in the city or town
C. residence: a person's home
D. public: all the people who live in a city

A city has many buildings which are open to the

_____. These buildings are kept clean
and in good repair by people who work for the

city. A _____ is not a public building. It is
a private building which is found in the

_____ part of the city. All _____
must take care of their own homes.

2 Practice With Content Words

DIRECTIONS Read the story. Use the story to figure out the definitions of the boldfaced words. Write the correct word under its definition.

Matt and his family moved from a small town in the country to a **suburb** of Chicago. Matt missed his old home, but he couldn't wait to visit the city.

One afternoon, Matt and his parents went into the city. They left the car at the **city limits** and boarded a bus. Matt enjoyed seeing the factories in the **industrial section.** In the **commercial section,** he saw his parents' offices and many large stores. Matt saw many different kinds of restaurants, with food from different countries. He was anxious to try all the **ethnic** foods.

When they reached the **civic center,** Matt saw a poster about a boat show that would be there next month. He thought that would be fun. Matt hoped he would visit the city often.

1. smaller city near a large one

   _____

2. part of a city where factories are found

   _____

3. building where special events are held

   _____

4. part of a city with offices and stores

   _____

5. boundary where a city starts

   _____

6. from a particular country

   _____

DIRECTIONS Read the story about how people work together to make a city a good place to live and work.

A city has schools, churches, banks, stores, a library and post offices. Major cities usually have hospitals and public transportation systems. Public transportation, like railroads, buses, cabs, and subways, can carry many people at a time from one place to another. Very large cities may have museums, art galleries, and civic centers, where large numbers of people attend sports events, meetings, or concerts.

The most important thing a city can have is people. Every city is made up of people who live and work together. A city may have thousands or millions of residents. Some people may work in the city but live in its suburbs.

Citizens of a city vote for leaders whose job is to make sure the city is a good place to live and work. The city government usually includes a mayor and a group of men and women who serve on the city council. The leaders have meetings to make decisions for the city. People who work in a city government have offices in a special public building called the city hall. The police and fire departments often have stations near city hall.

There are many jobs to be done in a city. Some people work to make sure the public transportation operates well. Other people build and repair the city streets. People who work in the sanitation department make sure water and food are safe. They also see that garbage and sewage are properly disposed of.

Cities have industrial, commercial and residential sections. The industrial area has many factories. Offices and stores are found in the commercial section of the city. People live in the residential sections. City governments plan special housing for some of its people. Senior citizen housing is provided for a city's older residents. Other housing is planned and maintained for people who otherwise would have no place to live.

DIRECTIONS Use the words you have learned about cities to answer the questions.

1. Is the mayor's office in a public or private building?

   _____

2. Where might some grandparents live in a larger city?

   _____

3. What kind of meeting would Sean's mother attend if she helps make decisions in the city government?

   _____

4. In which area of a city might truck tires be made?

   _____

5. What building in a city houses the mayor's office?

   _____

6. Name four kinds of public transportation.

   _____ _____

   _____ _____

7. In which department does Mr. Walker work if he checks water quality?

   _____

8. Which two words may be used to name a person who lives in a city?

   _____ _____

9. Which area of a city would have stores and offices?

   _____

10. What do people do to get city leaders?

   _____

REMEMBER Stories about cities have a special vocabulary.

State Nicknames

Some people like to use names which are less formal than their real ones. Bill is a nickname for William. Both names stand for the same person. In this lesson, you will read about states and their nicknames. You will learn words which, like nicknames, share their meanings with other words.

 KEYS to Synonyms

Synonyms are words that mean almost the same thing.

LEARN When two words mean almost the same thing, they are called synonyms. Synonyms can take the place of each other in a sentence.

EXAMPLE Elizabeth went with Grandma to the movie.
Liz went with Nannie to the film.
Elizabeth and *Liz* are synonyms.
So are *Grandma* and *Nannie* and *movie* and *film*.

DIRECTIONS Read each word. Write its letter beside its synonym.

A. Nick	**B.** street	**C.** Phil	**D.** Tom
E. Gramps	**F.** called	**G.** Bobbie	**H.** right

_____ **1.** Thomas   _____ **2.** Roberta   _____ **3.** Philip

_____ **4.** named   _____ **5.** correct   _____ **6.** Nicholas

_____ **7.** Grandfather   _____ **8.** pavement

Practice With Synonyms

DIRECTIONS Some words, like some names, may have several synonyms. Circle all the words in each row that are synonyms. (Hint: Make up a sentence using one synonym. If another word will fit in the sentence without changing the meaning, that word is probably a synonym.)

1. Patricia	Pat	Penny	Patty	Tricia
2. laughed	giggled	frowned	chuckled	chortled
3. home	people	house	room	thing
4. cats	persons	people	humans	alive
5. cloth	bonnet	fabric	place	material
6. go	stop	cease	halt	fall
7. save	discard	keep	waste	collect
8. knob	shape	leg	handle	door
9. Robert	Bill	Bob	Rob	Bobby
10. buy	gift	hook	present	belt
11. get	give	new	home	receive
12. town	road	highway	place	street
13. game	picture	prize	globe	reward
14. cold	hungry	starving	silly	need

Read and Apply

DIRECTIONS Read to find out how some states got their nicknames.

Some states take their nicknames from things that happened. Colorado is called the Centennial State because it became a state in the year the United States celebrated its hundredth birthday.

North Carolina became known as the Tarheel State because of a battle during the Civil War. Some soldiers from North Carolina were supposed to guard a hill. Troops from the North pushed them back. The soldiers from Mississippi laughed at them. They told the North Carolina soldiers to put tar on their heels next time. Then they would stick to the hill. They would not retreat again.

In 1889, the President of the United States said that settlers could have unowned land in the Oklahoma Territory. About 50,000 pioneers waited at the border for a rifle shot. The rifle shot would tell them it was time to race across the land and stake their claims. Some people were in too much of a hurry to wait for the shot. They wanted a head start. These people were called Sooners because they left sooner than they should have. When Oklahoma became a state, it was called the Sooner State.

Other states take their nicknames from nature. Idaho is called the Gem State because its land has so many precious stones. Arizona is called the Copper State because of all its copper mines. Ohio is called the Buckeye State because of its many Buckeye trees.

Alaska has an unusual name. It is called the Midnight Sun State. In the summertime, the earth is tilted so the sun stays out most of the time. People in Alaska can play baseball at midnight without any lights.

The sentences below come from the story you just read. Only the underlined word has been changed. Find the sentence in the story. Write the synonym for the underlined word on the line.

1. Ohio is called the Buckeye State because of its <u>numerous</u> Buckeye trees.

    _____

2. In 1889, the President of the United States said <u>pioneers</u> could have unowned land in the Oklahoma Territory.

    _____

3. Some soldiers told the North Carolina soldiers to put <u>pitch</u> on their heels next time.

    _____

4. Idaho is <u>nicknamed</u> the Gem State because its land has so many precious stones.

    _____

5. The rifle shot would tell them it was time to <u>scurry</u> across the land and stake their claims.

    _____

6. Some states take their nicknames from things that <u>occurred</u>.

    _____

7. In the summertime, the earth is <u>tipped</u> so the sun stays out most of the time.

    _____

8. Some soldiers from North Carolina were supposed to <u>protect</u> a hill.

    _____

REMEMBER Synonyms have similar meanings.

Backwards Day

If you walk in through a door marked *exit,* you are doing the opposite of what the sign tells you. In this lesson, you will read about words and ideas that are opposites. You will use opposites to change serious sentences into strange ones, or to do just the opposite.

 ## KEYS to Antonyms

Antonyms are words with opposite meanings.

LEARN Changing one or two words in a sentence can change the whole meaning.

> The proud dog pranced across the yard.
> The humble dog crawled across the yard.

What pictures did you see in your mind as you read the sentences? The two sentences paint different pictures because of the antonyms. *Proud* and *humble* have opposite meanings. So do *pranced* and *crawled.*

DIRECTIONS Read the words in the columns. Write the letter of the correct antonym in front of the word on the left.

_____ **1.** heated   **A.** weird   _____ **5.** repaired   **A.** end

_____ **2.** normal   **B.** cooled   _____ **6.** subtracted   **B.** added

_____ **3.** young   **C.** defeat   _____ **7.** begin   **C.** withdraw

_____ **4.** victory   **D.** aged   _____ **8.** deposit   **D.** broke

Practice With Antonyms

DIRECTIONS Have you ever played *Backwards Day?* On Backwards Day, everything you say is the opposite of what you really mean. Play Backwards Day with the sentences. Use an antonym from the box to replace each underlined word. Give each sentence its opposite meaning.

impatient	crunchy
youthful	departed
real	sturdy
filthy	sluggish
dry	powerful
bored	expanded

1. I was <u>excited</u> when Dad showed me the new bike.

2. The birds <u>arrived</u> when the weather got cold.

3. The winner was a <u>swift</u> runner.

4. The crying toddler was <u>patient</u>.

5. It is <u>humid</u> in the jungle.

6. Sometimes my big brother acts very <u>ancient</u>.

7. I like my cereal to be <u>soggy</u>.

8. He is sure that unicorns are <u>imaginary</u>.

9. A glass toy would not be <u>fragile</u>.

10. Ann polished her shoes to make them <u>spotless</u>.

11. You'll find that the giant is quite <u>weak</u>.

12. My jogging suit has <u>shrunk</u>.

DIRECTIONS Read the poem about two men whose names are antonyms. Imagine you are Mr. Tall and then Mr. Small as you read the poem about two characters who see the world from opposite views.

Mr. Tall and Mr. Small

Said Mr. Tall and Mr. Small,
"I see a skyscraper,
And a kite flying high
Made of crimson paper."

Said Mr. Small,
"I don't see any such things at all.
But I do see a ball
Rolling away behind a wall."

Cried Mr. Tall,
"Look what I found—
A bird's nest up in the old elm
    tree."

Replied Mr. Small,
"As for me,
I just found an acorn on the
    ground."

"The top of a mast,"
Espied Mr. Tall.
"Caboose chugging last,"
Vied Mr. Small.

"Upon my word,"
Announced Mr. Tall,
"There's a giraffe."

Don't be absurd,"
Pounced Mr. Small,
"It's a baby calf."

"Flagpoles," said Mr. Tall.
"Moles," said Mr. Small,
"In holes."

Said Mr. Tall,
"I see clouds that pass
All billowing pink,
Like a pillow for sleep."

Said Mr. Small,
"I'll take, I think,
A nap on the grass,
Green velvet deep."

—Eve Merriam

Read the sentences. Think of an antonym for each underlined word. Write it on the line.

1. I see a kite flying <u>high</u>. _____

2. I don't see those things at <u>all</u>. _____

3. I see a ball rolling <u>away</u> from me. _____

4. I found a bird's nest <u>down</u> there. _____

5. It's in the <u>old</u> elm tree. _____

6. I <u>found</u> an acorn on the ground. _____

7. I see the <u>top</u> of a mast. _____

8. I see a caboose chugging <u>last</u>. _____

9. I see clouds that <u>go</u> past. _____

10. I would rather be <u>asleep</u>. _____

11. I want to <u>take</u> a nap. _____

12. The pond is blue and <u>deep</u>. _____

REMEMBER Antonyms have opposite meanings.

A New Pet

Do you have a pet? Have you ever wanted one? In this lesson, you will read about a boy who wants a new pet. You will learn about some words that, like your pet, can play tricks on you.

KEYS to Homonyms

Homonyms are different words that sound the same.

LEARN   Some words sound the same but have different spellings and meanings. These words are called homonyms. *Pear* and *pair* sound the same. So do *flour* and *flower*. It's important to choose the right homonym. How would you like to eat a cake made from *flower*?

Read the pairs of homonyms in the box. Say the words to yourself. Do they sound the same? Do they mean the same thing? Pay attention to their spellings.

sent	nose	hear	dear	board
cent	knows	here	deer	bored

DIRECTIONS Choose one pair of homonyms from the box. Write each homonym on a line. Use it in a sentence.

1. _____ : _____
   (Homonym)   (Sentence)

2. _____ : _____
   (Homonym)   (Sentence)

DIRECTIONS Read the homonyms in the box. Read each pair of sentences. Choose the correct pair of homonyms for each pair of sentences. Write the correct homonym on the line. You may use a dictionary.

| blue | tail | eight | rap | right | bored |
| blew | tale | ate | wrap | write | board |

1. a. Carolyn went to _____ on the neighbor's door.

  b. Carolyn will _____ the present.

2. a. Marie _____ too much for lunch.

  b. Marie has _____ cents in her pocket.

3. a. Perry knew he had the _____ answer.

  b. Perry decided to _____ to his grandmother.

4. a. Henry's dog likes to wag its _____ .

  b. Henry's teacher read a fairy _____ to the class.

5. a. Martha and Chuck asked Dad for an old _____ .

  b. Martha and Chuck were _____ by the TV show.

6. a. Jenny _____ on the pinwheel to make it spin.

  b. Jenny has a new _____ bicycle.

DIRECTIONS Read about Henry Huggins and his new pets. Use the underlined words to answer the questions on the next page.

Every afternoon after school Ribsy waited for Henry under a <u>fir</u> tree in the corner of the school yard. Four days a <u>week</u> they ran home the shortest <u>way</u>, past the park, up the hill, and through the vacant lot.

On Fridays, however, they walked home the long way past the Lucky Dog Pet Shop. At the pet store, they stopped while Henry bought dog food from Mr. Pennycuff.

Henry liked to go to the pet store. The windows were full of puppies and kittens and, just before Easter, rabbits and baby chicks and ducks. Inside there was usually a parrot or a monkey, and once there had been a deodorized skunk.

Best of all Henry liked the fish. <u>One</u> side of the store was covered with <u>rows</u> of little tanks. Each aquarium contained green plants that grew underwater, snails, and a different kind of tropical fish. Henry always stopped to look into each tank. Mr. Pennycuff explained that the fish came from all over the world, but most of them came from jungle rivers <u>where</u> the water was warm. That was why they were called tropical fish.

One Friday when Henry went to the pet store, he saw a sign that <u>read</u>:

SPECIAL OFFER
- 1 PAIR OF GUPPIES
- FISH BOWL
- 1 SNAIL
- AQUATIC PLANT
- PACKAGE OF FISH FOOD

ALL FOR 79¢

"Jeepers!" said Henry. "All that for seventy-nine cents." He looked at the fish in the bowls. Each bowl held one <u>plain</u> silvery-gray fish almost two inches long and one smaller fish with all the colors of the rainbow. "That really is a bargain!"

"It certainly is," agreed Mr. Pennycuff. "Shall I <u>wrap</u> up a pair for you?"

Henry felt around in his pocket. The dollar his grandfather had given him was still there. He decided he had to have a pair of guppies. He would keep them on the dresser in his room. They would just stay in his room and swim quietly around in their bowl. He didn't see how his mother could object to two quiet little fish that didn't bark or track in mud or anything.

DIRECTIONS Use words from the story to answer the questions.

Find the homonym for . . .

1. <u>fur</u> that means "a kind of evergreen tree."

   _____

2. <u>plane</u> that means "not decorated."

   _____

3. <u>rap</u> that means "to fold a covering around."

   _____

4. <u>red</u> that means "had a particular meaning."

   _____

5. <u>rose</u> that means "things arranged in a straight line."

   _____

6. <u>weak</u> that means "a period of seven days."

   _____

7. <u>wear</u> that means "in what place."

   _____

8. <u>weigh</u> that means "a particular route or direction."

   _____

9. <u>won</u> that means "a single thing or unit."

   _____

REMEMBER Homonyms have the same sound, but different spellings and meanings.

Word Weaving

A weaver weaves together single strands to make a piece of cloth. A writer weaves words together to make a paragraph. The way words fit together to show the author's meaning is called context. In this lesson, you will use context to find word meaning. You will read about the largest bird in the world.

 ## KEYS to Context

The context is the way words fit together to give meaning.

LEARN   What do you do when you come across a word you don't know? Do you look it up or ask for help? First try using context to figure out the meaning. When you use the context, you look at the other words in the sentence. Sometimes you can find clues in the sentences that come before or after the difficult word.

DIRECTIONS Read each sentence. Write the number of the correct sentence on the line beside the definition of the underlined word.

1. Some people believe ostriches are <u>timid</u> birds who hide their heads in the sand when they sense danger.

2. Because an ostrich has <u>keen</u> eyesight, it can see enemies when they are still far away.

_____ **A.** acute, sharp, or sensitive   _____ **B.** fearful, lacking in courage or self-confidence

DIRECTIONS Read each paragraph. Use context to find the meaning of each underlined word. Circle the letter of its definition.

1. An Ostrich is a <u>colossal</u> bird. It is the largest bird in the world. Male ostriches grow to be about 8 feet tall and weigh over 300 pounds. The females are just a little smaller.

   <u>Colossal</u> tells about the ostriches'
   a. color. **b.** size. **c.** shape.

2. Most ostriches live in South Africa, but not all ostriches are wild. People in South Africa raise <u>domestic</u> ostriches. These tame ostriches are raised on farms like chickens or turkeys.

   <u>Domestic</u> tells how ostriches
   a. eat. **b.** run. **c.** live.

3. In the wild, ostriches live in large groups. They are very <u>social</u> animals. Several hundred ostriches often join together and live peacefully.

   <u>Social</u> animals live
   a. alone. **b.** in the wild.
   c. in groups.

DIRECTIONS Write a sentence for each of the underlined words. Write about something besides ostriches.

1. _____

   _____

2. _____

   _____

3. _____

   _____

Read and Apply

DIRECTIONS Read to find out about ostrich families. Some words may be new to you. Use context clues to help with the meanings.

Ostriches raise large families. One male lives with several females. It is his job to find a territory for himself and his family. He becomes very angry and protective if another male bird comes near his home ground. If another male wants the territory, the two males will battle. The winner claims his territory and works with his mates to build a nest.

Ostrich nests are not very deep, but they can be eight feet wide. The ostriches scrape a large hole in the ground for the nest. When the nest is ready, each female lays between six and ten eggs. Sometimes there can be as many as forty eggs in one nest. Each egg weighs about three pounds. As soon as the females have laid the eggs, the male takes over. His job is to incubate the eggs. He uses his beak to push the eggs under his warm body. When the nest is full of eggs, the male and the females will take turns keeping them warm.

Ostrich chicks hatch in about five or six weeks. The newly-hatched chicks are about a foot tall. They have spots and are a brownish-gray color. They look like puffy balls of grass. They blend in with their grassy home. Still, predators seem to find them. Many times a parent will come to the rescue and save a chick from being eaten.

Baby ostriches will grow to be as large as their parents. They will eat grasses, berries, insects, and even rodents. Since all this food must be ground up in the birds' gizzards, they must eat sand and gravel, too. The sand and gravel help to crush the food so it can be digested.

A full-grown ostrich cannot fly, but it can run swiftly. It uses its long legs to take huge steps. It can run between thirty-five and forty miles per hour. In some parts of South Africa, the people enjoy ostrich races. These are similar to horse races, with an ostrich taking the place of a horse.

DIRECTIONS Use context clues from the story to find the meaning of each underlined word. Write the correct letter on the line.

1. A territory is a ____.
   a. place
   b. nest
   c. mate

2. Incubate means ____.
   a. to push eggs gently
   b. to keep eggs warm
   c. to lay eggs

3. A predator lives by eating ____.
   a. seeds and nuts
   b. wild berries
   c. other animals

4. A bird's gizzard is like a ____.
   a. wing
   b. leg
   c. stomach

5. Swiftly means ____.
   a. slowly
   b. quickly
   c. in a straight line

REMEMBER Context clues help with difficult words.

The Unwelcome Gerbils

A chameleon makes a good pet. The small lizard can change its color to blend in with its surroundings. In this lesson, you will learn some words that can change their meanings to fit in with the words around them.

1 KEYS to Multiple-Meaning Words

The meaning of some words depends on the words around them.

EXAMPLE Cinderella lost her slipper at the *ball*.
The pitcher threw the *ball* over home plate.

LEARN The word *ball* has two different meanings in these sentences. In the first sentence, *ball* means "a dance or a party." In the second sentence, *ball* means "a round object for throwing." The meaning of *ball* is clear when you read the whole sentence.

DIRECTIONS Read each definition. Then read the sentences. Write the letter of the correct sentence beside the definition.

1. not course and heavy ____
   a. Floyd had to pay his library <u>fine</u>.
   b. Beth's hair is long and <u>fine</u>.

2. a connected line of railway cars ____
   a. The <u>train</u> was filled with passengers.
   b. Karla will <u>train</u> her dog to do tricks.

3. a small enclosure for animals ____
   a. The farmer kept his pigs in a <u>pen</u>.
   b. We are not allowed to use a <u>pen</u> in math class.

2 Practice With Multiple-Meaning Words

DIRECTIONS In each pair of sentences, the nonsense word *snizzle* has been substituted for the same multiple-meaning word. Write the word that can replace *snizzle* on the line.

1. The seeds were planted in the moist *snizzle*.
We could smell the freshly *snizzle* coffee.

_____

2. The ball began to *snizzle* down the hill.
Mom had a(n) *snizzle* and juice for breakfast.

_____

3. Divide the pie into a(n) *snizzle* number of pieces.
If you make the next basket we will be *snizzle*.

_____

4. My *snizzle* clock will go off at 7 o'clock.
The flooding river caused much *snizzle* in the village.

_____

5. Mother asked Mark to *snizzle* the hedge.
After his diet, Dad looked very *snizzle*.

_____

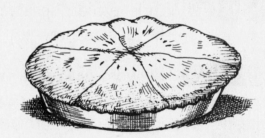

DIRECTIONS Print the first letter of each multiple-meaning word in order on the lines. Then you will know how you've done on this page.

___ ___   ___ ___   ___

Read and Apply

DIRECTIONS Read the story. Think about how you might convince your parents that you need a pet.

"Mom!" shouted Anastasia as she clattered up the back steps and into the kitchen after school. "Guess what Meredith Halberg gave me! Just what I've been wanting! And it didn't cost *anything!*"

Mrs. Krupnik put a casserole into the oven, closed the oven door, and adjusted the temperature. She turned around. "Let me think," she said. "Chicken pox?"

Anastasia made a face. It was terrible, having a mother who always made jokes. "Ha ha, very funny," she said. "I said it was something I'd been *wanting.* Anyway, I had chicken pox years ago."

"Well," said her mother, "I can't think of anything else that doesn't cost anything."

Anastasia was so excited she was almost jumping up and down. "You'll never guess! Wait, I'll show you. They're on the back porch. They're probably getting cold. I'll bring them in."

"Hold it," her mother said. She looked suspicious. "What do you mean, they're getting cold? It's not something *alive*, is it!"

But Anastasia had already gone, banging the door behind her. In a minute she was back, holding a wooden box with a wire mesh cover over it. A rustling sound came from the inside of the box.

Her mother retreated instantly, behind the kitchen table.

"No!" she said. "It is something alive! Anastasia, absolutely not! I've told you and told you that I can't stand—"

Anastasia wasn't listening. Her mother was so boring sometimes. She undid the latch and lifted the cover of the box.

"Gerbils!" she announced with delight.

Her mother backed away until she was against the refrigerator. She picked up a wooden spoon and held it like a weapon. "GET THOSE THINGS OUT OF MY KITCHEN IMMEDIATELY!" she bellowed.

DIRECTIONS Help Anastasia convince her mother she needs those gerbils. Read each incomplete sentence. Read the definition under the blank line. Think of a word that fits the definition and also makes the sentence make sense. Write a word on the line to complete the sentence.

1. I promise I'll always keep my gerbils in their _____ .

(fight with fists)

2. They won't _____ loose in the house.

(a point scored in baseball)

3. Gerbils are fun to _____ .

(clock worn on the arm)

4. I can _____ them to be good.

(line of railway cars)

5. "_____ , all right," said Mom.

(Deep hole filled with water)

REMEMBER The sentence tells you what multiple-meaning words mean.

The Croco-bus

Danny knows the meaning of the word *beat*. In fact, he knows too many meanings for *beat*. What should Danny do to the eggs? Which meaning should he choose? In this lesson, you will read about a crocodile who takes a bus ride. You will learn to choose the correct meaning for words with many meanings.

1 KEYS to Multiple-Meaning Words

Multiple-meaning words have more than one definition.

LEARN If a word has more than one meaning, you need to choose the correct definition. The rest of the sentence can help you decide. Read the dictionary entry for *beat*. What is the number of the meaning that tells what Danny is supposed to do?

> **beat** (bēt) *v.* **1** to hit or strike again and again; pound **2** to mix by stirring with a fork, spoon, or beater **3** to win over; defeat

DIRECTIONS Read each sentence. Write the number of the best meaning for *beat* on the line in front of the sentence.

_____ **a.** Sue beat her big brother at checkers.

_____ **b.** The falling acorns kept beating against the roof.

Practice With Multiple-Meaning Words

DIRECTIONS Read the sentences. Then read the definitions on the right. Choose the definition that is the best meaning for each underlined word. Write its letter on the line above the number of the correct sentence. If you are correct, the letters will spell out what you just did.

1. We couldn't wait to run in the big marathon.

   U. a cutting tool with a thin metal blade

2. Joe helped set the table.

   J. to aim one's finger at

3. Dad had to use a large saw to cut up the fallen limb.

   P. a sharp tip

4. Nancy broke the point of her pencil.

   B. used the sense of sight

5. Joan was a hero because she hit the winning run.

   S. to put in a certain place or position

6. The leaping puppy caused a run in Mrs. Jones' stocking.

   O. to become rigid, firm, or fixed

7. "When I point to you, say your line," said the director.

   E. a point scored in baseball by touching all the bases

8. The jello had to set for four hours to become solid.

   R. a place in knitted material where threads come apart

9. "I saw it first!" yelled Greg.

   A. to take part in a race

```
___  ___  ___  ___  ___  ___  ___  ___  ___
 1    2    3    4    5    6    7    8    9
```

DIRECTIONS Read the story. Pay special attention to the words in boldfaced type. Each one has more than one meaning.

"We can't take a crocodile on the bus, Harriet," said Anthea anxiously.

"Nonsense," said Harriet, **hitching** up her wriggling schoolbag.

Harriet's schoolbag didn't usually wriggle. It was wriggling this time because there was a crocodile inside it, eating.

The crocodile was a smallish, friendly crocodile. He had been pottering around in his cage at the zoo when Harriet whistled at him. The next thing he knew, he was inside Harriet's schoolbag, nestling up to her lunch box and eating her notebook. By the time Harriet reached the bus stop, he had eaten her math book and her pencil case, and was making a start on her beret.

"Now what do we do with it?" Anthea asked, standing on the side of Harriet which was farthest from the wriggling schoolbag.

"Take it home," said Harriet.

Harriet went back to whistling at her crocodile. She was a good whistler. Her whistle soothed the little crocodile. He stopped wriggling and **swallowed** the last shreds of the beret. As long as Harriet kept whistling, he was a happy crocodile.

The bus came. Harriet and Anthea got on and went to sit in the back.

"Stop that whistling!" shouted the conductor toward the back.

Harriet stopped. Her schoolbag started wriggling. Harriet started again.

"Stop that whistling," the conductor said, **advancing** down the aisle. "This is my bus and I won't have whistling on it."

Harriet shrugged and stopped whistling.

The schoolbag gave a gentle wriggle.

"What's that?" said the conductor, pointing at Harriet's wriggling schoolbag. With each wriggle, it was **inching** its way across the seat.

"My schoolbag," said Harriet.

Harriet grabbed at the strap and **pursed** her mouth to whistle, in the hope that the crocodile would stop wriggling.

"You've got an animal in that!" said the conductor. "No animals allowed on my bus without special permission. I won't have it!"

He grabbed the wriggling schoolbag and held it aloft.

"You're caught!" he cried triumphantly.

The boys who were sitting behind them took one look at the schoolbag and one look at Harriet and got off.

"I saw teeth," one of them muttered, as he backed away.

DIRECTIONS Find the sentence in the story that contains a form of each word. Use the whole sentence to decide which meaning applies. Write the correct letter on the line.

_____ **1.** advance
  a. to go forward; move ahead
  b. to cause to happen sooner

_____ **2.** hitch
  a. a knot that can be easily untied
  b. to move with a quick tug or jerk

_____ **3.** inch
  a. a unit for measuring length
  b. to move a little at a time

_____ **4.** purse
  a. to draw tightly together; pucker
  b. a sum of money given as a prize

_____ **5.** swallow
  a. a small swift-flying bird with a forked tail
  b. to get food from the throat to the stomach

REMEMBER Use clues in the sentence to choose the right meaning.

Visiting Scotland

When you travel, it's nice to know some shortcuts to get where you want to go. Sometimes when you read, you run across words that are shortcut words. In this lesson, you will take a trip to Scotland. You will learn to make sense of shortcut words called contractions.

 1 KEYS to Contractions

Contractions are a combination of two separate words.

LEARN   A contraction is made by taking some letters out of one of the words it stands for and replacing them with an apostrophe. This is true of almost every contraction. One contraction changes even more. That contraction is *won't*. *Won't* stands for *will not*.

When you come to a contraction in your reading, you may need to figure out which two words it stands for before the sentence makes sense.

EXAMPLE   I'll = I will   where's = where is   I've = I have

DIRECTIONS Read the sentences. Underline the contraction. Write the number of the sentence beside the two words the contraction stands for.

1. Let's take a trip to Scotland. _____ **a.** will not

2. That's where the Loch Ness
   Monster lives. _____ **b.** let us

3. Maybe we won't visit Nessie. _____ **c.** that is

DIRECTIONS Read each sentence. Underline the two words that can be made into a contraction. Write the contraction on the line.

1. Our class decided we would take an imaginary trip to Scotland.

   _____

2. It is a country just north of England.

   _____

3. We had never been to Scotland before.

   _____

4. The trip will not take long.

   _____

5. We will go there in our minds.

   _____

6. There will be many things to see in Scotland.

   _____

7. Most of us do not believe in the Loch Ness monster.

   _____

8. Everyone would have enjoyed trying to spot it anyway.

   _____

9. We could not find any men wearing plaid kilts.

   _____

10. We could have bought some beautiful sweaters.

    _____

11. We will not forget the strange sound of the bagpipes.

    _____

12. Maybe we will really go to Scotland some day.

    _____

3

Read and Apply

DIRECTIONS Read the story. Underline the contractions. Write each contraction and the two words it stands for on the lines beside the story.

When Jane walked into class, Rita was waiting for her.

"There's a new student in our class," she said excitedly. "He's over there by Mr. Willets."

The new student was named Duncan. When he started to speak, everyone knew he wasn't from anywhere near.

"We know you're speaking English, but we don't recognize your accent," Pete said.

Duncan laughed.

"I think it's you who have the accent," he said. "But you are right. I haven't been in this country long. I've lived in Scotland all my life. I'm spending the year with my grandparents."

"What's it like to live in Scotland?" asked Jane.

1. _____ = _____ + _____

2. _____ = _____ + _____

3. _____ = _____ + _____

4. _____ = _____ + _____

5. _____ = _____ + _____

6. _____ = _____ + _____

7. _____ = _____ + _____

8. _____ = _____ + _____

9. _____ = _____ + _____

10. _____ = _____ + _____

Finish the story. Underline the contractions. Write the contraction and the two words it stands for.

"Life in Scotland isn't so different from life here," answered Duncan. "We watch television, too. We like football, but our football is what you call soccer."

"There's some beautiful country in Scotland," Duncan continued. "When I get home we'll visit my cousins. They live in the highlands on a farm. My cousins raise sheep. They'll make beautiful sweaters from the wool. There's a real need for wool in Scotland. Our climate is cool all year long. It doesn't ever get hot."

"Why aren't you wearing a kilt?" asked Tim.

The class giggled. Duncan smiled.

"Men in Scotland do wear kilts," he said. "We only wear them on special occasions, though. I can do something to remind you of my country. I'm learning to play the bagpipes. I'll be glad to bring mine in tomorrow and play for you."

The bell rang. The students started toward their seats.

"We're going to have fun learning about Scotland," they said. "It's going to be sad when Duncan has to leave. It'll be fun having a friend in Scotland, though."

1. _____ = _____ + _____   7. _____ = _____ + _____

2. _____ = _____ + _____   8. _____ = _____ + _____

3. _____ = _____ + _____   9. _____ + _____ + _____

4. _____ = _____ + _____   10. _____ = _____ + _____

5. _____ = _____ + _____   11. _____ = _____ + _____

6. _____ = _____ + _____   12. _____ = _____ + _____

Mythical Creatures

How would you feel if you saw a creature with the head of an eagle and the body of a lion? You might think you were having a nightmare, because you know such a creature does not really exist. In ancient Greece people imagined that there actually were such creatures. They invented them to explain natural events, like fire and storms.

In this lesson, you will read about mythical creatures. You will learn about compound words.

1 KEYS to Compound Words

Compound words have two shorter words inside.

LEARN Just as mythical creatures were often made from more than one animal, compound words are made from more than one word. The word *nightmare* in the first paragraph is a compound word. The short words *night* and *mare* have been joined to make a new word.

EXAMPLE sunshine = sun + shine   airplane = air + plane

DIRECTIONS Make compound words by joining a word in the first column with a word in the second. Write the compound words on the lines.

room	place	_____
barn	ball	_____
foot	yard	_____
fire	mate	_____

Practice With Compound Words

DIRECTIONS Find a compound word to complete each sentence. Write it on the line.

classroom	airmail	bathroom	doorknob	baseball	headlight
raincoat	shoelace	girlfriend	grapefruit	mailbox	birthday

1. My _____ and I went to the movie.

2. You need a bat and a ball to play _____.

3. We are going to have a poetry writing contest in our _____.

4. Put the letters in the _____.

5. Sometimes I have _____ for breakfast.

6. My _____ is untied.

7. Turn the _____ to open the door.

8. There is no shower in that _____.

9. It looked cloudy, so Art wore his _____.

10. Janet wanted the package to get there quickly, so she sent it _____.

11. Two boys in Jon's class were born on the same _____.

12. My sister's car has a broken _____.

DIRECTIONS Read the story about creatures from Greek mythology. Pay special attention to the underlined words.

In ancient times people invented mysterious creatures to explain natural events they could not <u>understand</u>. Greek mythology is full of such creatures. They often had <u>supernatural</u> powers. <u>Sometimes</u> the creatures were part man and part beast. Sometimes they were a combination of two or more beasts.

The griffin was an <u>awesome</u> creature invented by the ancient Greeks. This monster had the head and wings of an eagle and the body of a lion. The griffin, they believed, came from the land of <u>sunshine</u>. It was his job to guard treasure. Imagine seeing one of these creatures at <u>nighttime</u>. You would not dare to steal any of its treasure!

The chimera (ki ′mirə) was a female monster of Greek mythology. She was indeed a <u>fearsome</u> creature. She had the head of a lion, the body of a shaggy goat, and the tail of a dragon. She breathed fire that scorched <u>farmland</u> and destroyed crops in the land of Lycia. Today the word *chimera* means any frightening thing of the imagination.

Pan was another mythical creature. He was part man and part goat. His body and head were those of a man, but he had the legs, tail and beard of a goat. Pan was god of the <u>woodlands</u>. He wandered through forests playing music on his <u>panpipe</u>, an instrument he made from hollow reeds. Sometimes his music frightened the animals and caused them to stampede. Although Pan was a friendly god, hunters and shepherds were often afraid of him. The word *panic* means an unreasonable fear. It comes from the name of the Greek god Pan.

DIRECTIONS Complete each sentence with a compound word from the story you just read. Write the correct compound on the line.

1. Pan was the Greek god of the

   _____.

2. Chimera destroyed the

   _____ of Lycia.

3. The griffin came from the land

   of _____.

4. The creatures would really be frightening at

   _____.

5. The ancient Greeks thought some creatures had

   _____ powers.

6. The _____ was a musical instrument.

7. Two words that describe mythical creatures are

   _____ and

   _____.

8. Mythical creatures were invented to explain events people could not

   _____.

9. _____ people were afraid of the gods.

REMEMBER A compound word is made from two shorter words.

Lost Dog

Have you ever had a pet that ran away for awhile? If you have, you know losing a pet can be upsetting. In this lesson, you will read about a girl who has lost her dog. You will learn to change a word's meaning by adding a prefix.

 ## KEYS to Prefixes

A prefix at the beginning of a word changes its meaning.

LEARN   A prefix is a group of letters added to the beginning of a word. Prefixes have special meanings. When a prefix is added to a word, the word's meaning changes.

EXAMPLE   *Re* means *to do again*. If you *re*read a story, you read it again.
   The prefix *un* makes a word mean just the opposite of what it meant before. If you are *un*comfortable, you are not comfortable.
   Dis also makes a word mean its opposite. If you *dis*agree, you do not agree.

DIRECTIONS Complete these sentences with *re, un,* or *dis*. The new word should have the meaning in the parentheses.

1. Do you _____ hamsters? (not like)

2. That ice is _____ for skating. (not safe)

3. We need to _____ the meatloaf. (heat again)

② Practice With Prefixes

DIRECTIONS Add *re, un,* or *dis,* to each underlined word. Write the new word on the line to complete the sentence.

1. <u>paint</u> We will _____ our house this spring.

2. <u>fair</u> It is _____ to cheat at games.

3. <u>agree</u> I do not _____ with what you said.

4. <u>like</u> I _____ getting up in the morning.

5. <u>plant</u> The farmer had to _____ his corn.

6. <u>write</u> Ken had to _____ his lost assignment.

7. <u>true</u> The tall tale sounds _____ to me.

DIRECTIONS The sentences below do not make sense. Add *un,* or *dis* to each word in boldface type to correct the sentence.

1. Children should not _____**obey** their parents.

2. Pierre was _____**happy** when he lost his toy truck.

3. A newborn baby is _____**able** to talk.

4. Diane always _____**ties** her shoes before she takes them off.

5. A person who fibs is _____**honest.**

6. The tot was hot and _____**comfortable** in the bright sunlight.

DIRECTIONS Read the story. Pay special attention to the underlined words.

Angela stepped off the school bus and looked toward her house.

"Where is Charlie?" she wondered.

Charlie was Angela's terrier. Ever since Angela's first day of school, Charlie had always raced to the bus to greet her. Today Charlie was nowhere to be seen. Angela ran up the steps of her house and into the den. Her mother was restitching a hem.

"Is Charlie with you?" Angela asked her mother.

"I haven't seen Charlie for a while," she said. "Have you called him? I'm sure he's around somewhere."

Angela called Charlie. She looked all around the yard. She even unlatched the garage door and went inside. Angela was very unhappy. It looked like Charlie was really lost.

"Mom," she said. "I'm really worried. I'm going to go look for Charlie."

"Good idea," answered Mom, "but don't go into the park alone."

Angela looked all over the neighborhood. She looked in front yards and back yards. Unable to find her dog, she retraced her steps. Angela did not want to disobey her mother, but she just had to find Charlie. She took a deep breath. She called Charlie once more. Then she crossed the street and entered the park.

Charlie was not in the park. Angela was really worried now. She was not just worried about Charlie. She knew her mother would be disappointed in her. She disliked coming home without Charlie, but there was nothing else to do.

Angela's mother was <u>displeased</u> with Angela.

"We all love Charlie," she said, "but we love you, too, and the park is not a safe place to be."

She told Angela to go to her room, <u>undress</u>, and go to bed. What an <u>unlucky</u> day! It all seemed so <u>unfair</u>. Charlie was gone and she was in big trouble. Angela cried herself to sleep.

In the middle of the night, she awoke with a start. What was that noise? She listened carefully. Then she heard it again. It was Charlie's bark. Her lost dog had <u>reappeared</u>. She saw the porch light go on. Her mother had been waiting up for Charlie. Suddenly Angela knew everything was all right.

DIRECTIONS Read each incomplete sentence. Find an underlined word in the story that will complete each sentence. Write it on the line.

1. Some people think it is

   _____ to walk under a ladder.

2. The moon

   _____ from behind the cloud.

3. Jim _____ his steps to look for his lost wallet.

4. I am _____ to read my grandmother's handwriting.

5. I will not _____ by staying out too late.

6. The babysitter had to

   _____ the baby and put him to bed.

7. Dad is _____ the seams of the broken tent.

8. I _____ the door and ran into the yard.

9. Sometimes we cry when we

   are _____ .

10. Mom was _____ when she saw the mess.

11. Our cat _____ getting his fur wet.

12. The softball coach thought the

    call was _____ .

REMEMBER Prefixes give words a new meaning.

Water Wise

How many times have you used water since you woke up this morning? Sometimes we take water for granted. In this lesson, you will read about the importance of water to all living things. You will learn to recognize words with suffixes.

KEYS to Suffixes

 1 **A suffix is a group of letters added to the end of a word.**

LEARN When you add a suffix to a base word, you form a new word.

vapor: a mass of tiny drops of water floating in air
vaporize: to change into vapor

Sometimes a suffix changes the spelling of a base word.

ice-icy drip-dripping pure-purify run-running

DIRECTIONS Read the base words and the new words made by adding suffixes. Circle the suffix in each new word.

1. help: h e l p s   h e l p e d   h e l p i n g
2. pollute: p o l l u t i o n p o l l u t e d   p o l l u t e s
3. use: u s i n g   u s e f u l   u s i n g
4. care: c a r e d   c a r e l e s s   c a r e s

DIRECTIONS Read the article. Pay special attention to words with suffixes.

We live in a world of water. Most of the water is in the ocean. Imagine you could put all the water in the world in 100 large glasses. Water from the ocean would fill 97 glasses.

It's easy to take for granted the water we get by turning the handle of a faucet. Water is in other places, too. Every living thing on earth is made mostly of water. Your body is two-thirds water. An elephant's body is even more than two-thirds water. A tomato is almost all water.

Water is more than liquid refreshment. No living organism can survive long without it. During your lifetime, you will take in about 16,000 gallons of water. Humans can live more than a month without food, but they would live less than a week without water.

DIRECTIONS Each base word below appears in the article with a suffix added. Find the words in the article. Write each word on the line beside its base word.

1. human _____

2. organ _____

3. live _____

4. turn _____

5. refresh _____

6. glass _____

7. most _____

8. hand _____

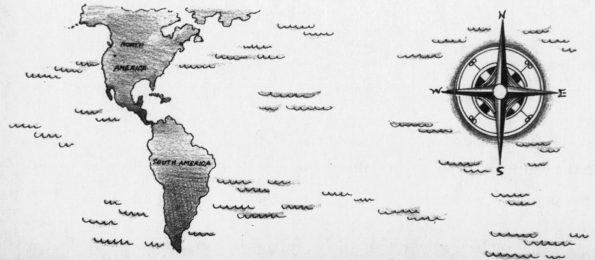

DIRECTIONS Read more about water. Watch for words with suffixes.

All water is found in one of three forms. It's easy to recognize water in its liquid form. That is the water you drink or swim in. Solid water is called ice or snow. Water in its liquid or solid form is visible. You can see it before or after freezing.

The third form of water is not so easily seen. This is water in the form of a gas. When water is a gas, it is called water vapor. It is invisible. Clouds and fog contain water vapor. People sometimes use vaporizers to add water vapor to the air. Additional water vapor in a room helps nighttime breathing.

Water is always in one of its three forms. It is always changing from one form to another. Think of an ice cube as water in its solid form. When it melts, it becomes water in its liquid form. If the liquid is left in the open air, it will evaporate. Then it becomes water in its gaseous form, or water vapor. The water cycle occurs all the time.

DIRECTIONS Find words with suffixes in the article. Use them to complete the sentences.

1. Water is _____ seen in its liquid and solid forms.

2. A _____ adds water vapor to the air.

3. Water is always

    _____ its form.

4. You can make solid water by

    _____ the liquid.

5. Water vapor is water in its

    _____ form.

Think about how water is used in your home. It is used for cooking, cleaning, and carrying waste away. A bath takes thirty to forty gallons of water. You brush your teeth with water. Washing your dirty dishes can take about ten gallons of water. One load of dirty clothes needs thirty to forty gallons of water to make it clean again. Some of your food is cooked in water. You use frozen water in iced drinks or frozen treats.

Water is used more than any other material in factories. Electricity is created with the use of water. Water provides recreation and transportation for people. Crops must be irrigated when rainfall is not plentiful.

Our need for water is steadily increasing as the number of people grows. If waste is thrown into rivers and lakes, the water becomes harmful to people, animals, and plants. Pollution and wasteful use of water threaten our water supply. At this moment scientists are studying ways to get more fresh water by making fresh water from salt water and by purifying unclean water. We can help conserve water by using water carefully.

DIRECTIONS Find a word in the story that is the given base word with a suffix added. Write it on the line beside the base word.

1. pollute _____

2. science _____

3. pure _____

4. transport _____

5. careful _____

6. make _____

7. provide _____

8. increase _____

9. steady _____

10. irrigate _____

11. electric _____

12. waste _____

13. plenty _____

14. dish _____

REMEMBER Long words are easier when you recognize suffixes.

Animal Comparisons

One way to learn about new things is to compare them with things you already know about. Look at the animal in the picture. How is it like animals you already know about? How is it different? What would you call this new animal?

In this lesson, you will learn to compare. You will look for ways that two things are alike. You will look for ways that they are different.

 ## KEYS to Comparisons

Comparing helps you understand new things.

LEARN When you compare two things, you think about how they are alike and how they are different. Making comparisons is one way to understand the world around us.

DIRECTIONS How are the animals in each sentence alike? How are they different? Use what you already know about animals to complete each sentence.

1. A duck is something like a goose, but a duck _____

_____

2. A cow is something like a horse, but a cow _____

_____

3. A goat is something like a deer because it _____

_____

② Practice With Comparisons

DIRECTIONS Now try a special kind of comparison called an analogy. Study the example.

EXAMPLE **Cow** is to **milk** as **hen** is to **eggs.**

In an analogy, the first two words in boldface type have the same relationship as the last two. That is, **cow** and **milk** are connected in the same way as **hen** and **eggs.** A cow gives us milk to drink. A hen gives us eggs to eat.

DIRECTIONS Complete the analogies. Follow the steps to help with number one. Then complete the next two by yourself.

1. Croak is to **frog** as **quack** is to

_____ .

Step 1: Ask yourself, "What is the relationship between croak and frog?" (A croak is the sound a frog makes.)
Step 2: Write a word on the line to complete the sentence. It should show the same relationship. (If you chose duck, good for you. Quack is the sound a duck makes.)

2. Bird is to **nest** as **bee** is to

_____ .

3. Whale is to **ocean** as **camel** is to

_____ .

Read and Apply

DIRECTIONS Read the poem about animal babies. Use what you learn to help you complete the analogies on page 52.

Animal babies are all shapes and sizes—
Plain, striped, or spotted, and full of surprises.
But one thing, you see,
Which seems funny to me,
Is that animal babies—gigantic or small—
Aren't really called babies at all.

A baby dog is called a pup.
A beaver's a pup, too, until it grows up.
And all baby seals have pup for a name.
That seems rather odd, for they just aren't the same.

Cats have kittens, all covered with fur,
Kittens that mew, kittens that purr-r-r-r.
Of all kinds of kittens, there's one that is funny.
Kitten's the name for a soft baby bunny.

A baby camel's a colt when it's new.
Some horses are colts when they are young, too.
Donkeys have colts.
So do zebras with stripes.
Colts are all babies of similar types.

Lions and tigers and bears may be wild,
But their babies, called cubs, are gentle and mild.
The high-yipping fox and the wolf with its howl
Also have cubs. So do sharks on the prowl.
The far-swimming walrus, the nicest of all,
Has babies called cubs while they are still small.

The babe of a cow is always called "calf,"
And so is the long-necked baby giraffe,
And calf is the name of a baby rhinoceros.
It's also the name of a young hippopotamus.
The elephant baby's a calf that's not small,
But the calf of a whale is largest of all.

DIRECTIONS Complete the analogies. Look back at the poem for help with some of the answers.

1. **Cat** is to **kitten** as **zebra** is to _____ .

2. **Owl** is to **hoot** as **crow** is to _____ .

3. **Person** is to **talk** as **dog** is to _____ .

4. **Dove** is to **coo** as **lion** is to _____ .

5. **Ant** is to **hill** as **spider** is to _____ .

6. **Dog** is to **pup** as **shark** is to _____ .

7. **Whale** is to **calf** as **walrus** is to _____ .

8. **Fox** is to **fur** as **snake** is to _____ .

9. **Rabbit** is to **warren** as **lion** is to _____ .

REMEMBER An analogy is a kind of comparison.

Hot Dog!

Do you enjoy making and eating good food? If you do, you know a recipe can help. If you follow the directions correctly, the food will taste good. In this lesson, you will practice following directions. You will read about a popular food—the hot dog.

1 KEYS to Following Directions

Read! Think! Do! Check!

LEARN   When you read the directions, pay close attention to the words that tell you what to do. Do the directions tell you to make a check, draw a circle, write on the line, draw a box around, or make an X?

Watch for words that tell you where to put the mark, like *under, around, on,* or *beside.*

DIRECTIONS Read the picnic menu. Then follow the directions.

1. Circle the dessert.
2. Put an X on the vegetable.
3. Underline the name of the drink.
4. Check the fruit.
5. Draw a box around the food
   you will read about in the story.

Apples
Hot Dogs
Carrot Sticks
Milk
Oatmeal Cookies

2 Practice Following Directions

DIRECTIONS Have you ever tried to put together something from a kit? If you have, you know how important it is to follow directions carefully. Follow the directions for drawing the side view of a hot dog dragster. Remember! Read all the directions first. Think about what the dragster will look like. Do what the directions tell you to do. Then check to see that you followed the directions correctly.

1. Draw hot dog bun in the center of the space for the car body.
2. Put a green olive with a red center on one end of the bun for a headlight.
3. Draw a round slice of onion where the windshield should be.
4. Put two slices of pickle where the wheels belong.

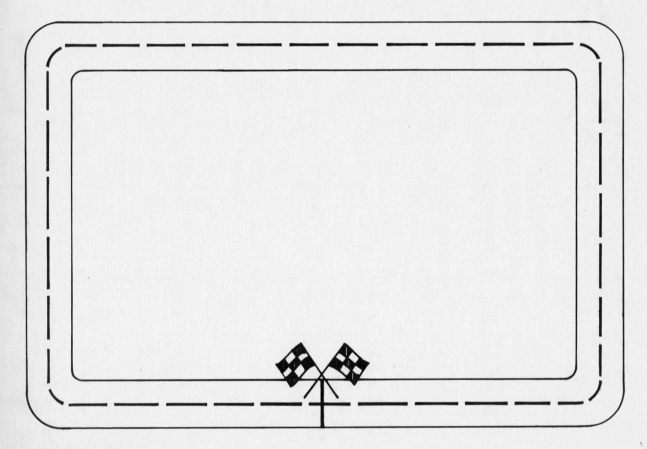

DIRECTIONS After you finish your drawing, follow the directions below.

A. Draw a line under your hot dog dragster.
B. Make a check mark beside the front wheel.
C. Put an X on the windshield.
D. Circle the headlight.

Read and Apply

DIRECTIONS Read the story to find out how the hot dog got its name. Use the story to help you follow the directions on page 56.

Many people love to eat hot dogs. Did you know that people in the United States alone eat over 14 billion hot dogs every year? Every second of the day 450 hot dogs are eaten. This means that, on the average, each person in the United States eats about 65 hot dogs a year.

Another name for the hot dog is *weiner*. The first weiner was probably served back in 1904. A man called a sausage vendor sold weiners from a cart on the street. He called the weiners "red hots." The "red hots" were too hot for people to touch and to eat. The vendor passed out white gloves so people would not burn their hands while they enjoyed their treat. One vendor thought of a great idea. He made a bun to fit the weiner. From that time on, no one ever needed white gloves again to enjoy a "red hot."

Maybe you have never heard anyone call a weiner a "red hot." That's because we are used to the name "hot dog." Some people think the hot dog got its name when a man called Harry Stevens was searching for some kind of good hot food to sell at football games. Mr. Stevens decided to try his luck at selling weiners in buns.

The shape of the weiners reminded him of the small dog with a long thin body called dachshund. To get the attention of the spectators, he told his sales boys to go out into the crowd and yell, "Get your red hot dachshund sausages!"

A sportswriter at one of the football games heard the boys yelling. He used the idea of a dachshund sausage to make up a cartoon character. The character he created was a talking sausage named "Hot Dog." From that time on weiners have been known as hot dogs.

DIRECTIONS Read, think, do, and check. Practice following directions.

1. Circle the number of hot dogs people in the United States eat every year.

2. Put an X on the year when people think the first hot dog was served.

3. Draw a line under the word that tells what people wore on their hands to protect them from the "red hots."

4. Make a check beside the name of the man who wanted to sell hot foods at football games.

5. Draw a box around the paragraph that tells about the cartoon that gave the hot dog its name.

REMEMBER Read, think, do, and check.

Big Now—Bigger Then

It's fun to visit a zoo and see interesting animals. You will see some animals that are very large. In this lesson, you will read about some large animals and their ancestors. You will learn about main ideas and details.

1 KEYS to Main Ideas and Details

A main idea tells what a paragraph is about. Details tell more about the main idea.

LEARN A paragraph has one important idea. That is its main idea. It is often the first sentence in a paragraph. All the other ideas are details that tell more about the main idea.

DIRECTIONS Read the paragraph. Find the main idea.

There are many large animals in the world today. A giraffe is so tall it can eat the leaves from the tops of trees. Snakes like the python and anaconda are so long they can stretch all the way across a four-lane highway. The albatross is a large bird. It is over ten feet from the tip of one wing to the other. The elephant is the largest animal that lives on land. A bull elephant can weigh up to six tons.

1. Circle the letter of the sentence that tells the main idea of the paragraph above.

   a. Giraffes are very tall animals.
   b. Many large animals live in the world today.
   c. It's a good idea to avoid large snakes.

DIRECTIONS Read the topic sentence. Circle the letter of each sentence that contains a detail that supports the main idea in the topic sentence. Write the new paragraph on the lines.

Topic sentence: Some animals that lived long ago were much bigger than any animal today.

a. Our tallest giraffe is short compared to the dinosaur called Tyrannosaurus Rex.

b. The smallest bird alive today is the hummingbird.

c. Some ancient birds had wings the size of a small airplane's wings.

d. Even our huge elephants would be dwarfed by their ancestor the mammoth.

e. Many people are afraid of snakes.

DIRECTIONS Read the paragraphs. On the lines below each paragraph, write the main idea and details. Write the main idea beside the Roman numeral. Write each detail beside a letter. Use your own words. Use phrases, not whole sentences.

A. Scientists found out about ancient animals by studying clues the animals left behind. One kind of clue is the fossil, which is the remains of an animal that has turned to stone. Sometimes the actual bones have been found buried in the earth. In the case of the ancient mammoth, whole bodies were preserved in ice in Russia. When the bodies were dug up, they looked just as they did when the animal died thousands of years ago.

B. The La Brea Tar Pits were a death trap for animals in ancient times. The tar pits were like lakes with sticky tar where the sand should be. Animals would walk into the water to take a drink. Their feet would get stuck in the sticky tar. Then the animal would die. When the tar pits dried up, the animal remains turned into fossils.

I. _____

_____

A. _____

B. _____

C. _____

_____

I. _____

A. _____

B. _____

C. _____

D. _____

E. _____

C. The job of the paleontologist is to make it possible for us to see dinosaurs today. Paleontologists go to places where dinosaur bones have been discovered. The scientists make sure the bones are carefully dug up. They assemble the bones like you would put a puzzle together. They put the bones in a museum so people can see them.

I. _____

   A. _____

   B. _____

   C. _____

   D. _____

REMEMBER Details explain the main idea.

The Legend of Never-Stop

There were no televisions in the old West. The pioneers entertained themselves by making up tall tales. In this lesson, you will read one of those tall tales. You will learn about main ideas and details.

1   KEYS to Main Idea and Details

The main idea is what the story is about. Details tell more about the main idea.

LEARN The main idea is the most important idea in what you read. The details are evidence that the main idea is true.

DIRECTIONS Read the beginning of the tall tale. Then read the sentences. Write MI in front of the sentence that tells the main idea. Write D before the sentences that tell details.

    Around the 1880s, there was quite a problem with fences in Texas. It seems the ranchers and the sheepherders had different ideas about boundary lines. Sometimes, tempers could get heated. If you wanted a fence, you didn't talk it over. You just went ahead and put it up. You got your supplies and crew together and went to work—the quicker, the better.

_____ **1.** People sometimes lost their tempers.

_____ **2.** Fences caused problems in Texas in the 1880s.

_____ **3.** People disagreed about boundaries.

_____ **4.** You tried to get your fence up before anyone knew about it.

Practice With Main Ideas and Details

DIRECTIONS Continue reading the story of Never-Stop. Then read the details that follow each underlined main idea. Fill in the blanks to complete each detail.

Nancy Owen had her mind set on fencing the border of her Texas ranch. She was stubborn, but not as stubborn as the hard and rocky ground on her ranch. No one seemed to be able to dig post holes fast enough to keep ahead of the fencing crew.

One morning a tall, thin stranger appeared at Miss Owen's door. His clothes and beard looked very different from anyone on the fence crew. He didn't seem to understand English or Spanish.

Nancy decided to try him at digging postholes. She couldn't talk to him, so she showed him what to do. She stepped off thirteen paces from the last posthole and picked up the shovel. Then she pointed straight south.

1. <u>Nancy wanted to fence her ranch.</u> The land was

   _____ and

   _____. No one could

   dig postholes _____

   _____.

2. <u>They knew he was a stranger.</u>

   His _____ and

   _____ were different. He

   couldn't speak _____

   or _____.

3. <u>Nancy wanted him to dig</u>

   postholes. She _____

   him what to do. She pointed to

   the _____.

DIRECTIONS Finish the story of Never-Stop. Then use the main ideas and details to answer the questions on the next page.

The stranger was not a Texan, but he sure could dig postholes. Like a flash he was out of sight of the fencing crew. He was so far ahead on the second day that Miss Owen had to ride out to check on him. By the end of the third day, no one could even find the hard-working posthole digger. All they could see were his postholes in a wonderful straight line. They were exactly thirteen paces apart and headed straight south.

Nobody ever did catch up with Never-Stop, the posthole digger. The fencing crew stopped at the end of Miss Nancy's ranch, but the postholes didn't. Miss Owen rode a day's ride further. The line of holes stretched on and on. She never did find the end.

To this day, no one is sure what happened to the stranger. On bright, moonlit nights, more than one lonesome traveler has reported seeing an old man with a flowing gray beard heading south. He holds a worn-out shovel no bigger than a wooden spoon. He always does the same thing. He walks thirteen paces. Then he stops and digs.

How well do you remember the main ideas and details? Circle the letter of the correct answers to the questions.

1. Where did the story take place?

   a. Tennessee
   b. Mexico
   c. Texas

2. Why did people call the stranger Never-Stop?

   a. He would never stop talking.
   b. He never stopped digging postholes.
   c. He was so tall, it looked like he would never stop.

3. Which description best fits the stranger?

   a. the man who digs forever
   b. the lazy posthole digger
   c. the big man on a horse

4. Why was it important to build a fence quickly?

   a. Your neighbors might stop you.
   b. Everyone else wanted a fence, too.
   c. The crew might charge more later.

5. Why was it hard to find a good posthole digger?

   a. Miss Nancy wasn't paying good wages.
   b. No one liked Miss Nancy.
   c. The ground was rocky and hard to dig.

6. Which sentence best tells the main idea of the whole story?

   a. If you wanted a fence, you put it up and talked later.
   b. To this day, no one is sure what happened to the stranger.
   c. The stranger didn't come from Texas or Mexico.

The Snowflake Man

Wilson Bentley's neighbors could be sure of one thing. Whenever it snowed, Bentley would rush outside. He just couldn't stay away from snowflakes. That's why they called him "Snowflake" Bentley. In this lesson, you will read about "Snowflake" Bentley, the first man to take a picture of a snowflake. You will learn about sequence.

KEYS to Sequence

Sequence is the order of events in a story.

LEARN Events are the things that happen in a story. The events happen in a certain order, or sequence. Some words are clues to the sequence of events. Read the words in the box. The words in the top row tell us something happened before something else. The words in the bottom row tell us something happened afterwards.

| before | early | first | in the beginning |
| later | after | next | finally |

DIRECTIONS Use the words in the box to help you circle the sentence that comes first in each pair.

1. **a.** Early in the day, the sky began to get cloudy.
   b. Later the snow began to fall.
2. **a.** Then Wilson raced out the door and down the street.
   b. First Wilson grabbed his coat.

DIRECTIONS Read the science activity. Then unscramble the steps. Number the steps to show the correct sequence.

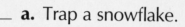

If it snows where you live, you can make a snowflake trap to study snowflakes. First collect the materials: a large piece of cardboard, a large piece of black cloth, a stapler, and a handlens. Cut the cardboard into a six inch (15 centimeter) square. Staple the black cloth to one side of the cardboard. Store your snowflake trap in the freezer. Sit back and wait for snow.

When the snow falls, take the trap out of the freezer. Take it outside right away. Let a few snowflakes land on the cloth. Then take your snowflake trap to a cold place that is out of the sun. Study the snowflakes through the handlens. Draw a picture of a snowflake. Notice how each snowflake is different.

_____ **a.** Trap a snowflake.

_____ **b.** Try to draw a picture of a snowflake.

_____ **c.** When snow falls, take the trap outside right away.

_____ **d.** Use a handlens to study the snowflakes.

_____ **e.** Collect the materials.

_____ **f.** Staple the cloth to the cardboard.

_____ **g.** Cut the cardboard into a square.

_____ **h.** Take the trap to a cold, sheltered place.

_____ **i.** Put the snowflake trap in the freezer.

A. It was pure chance that Wilson Bently got interested in snowflakes. One day his mother surprised him with a microscope. After that, you could always find him looking into things. One winter day, he took the microscope outside. Soon snowflakes began to fall. Some of them landed on the glass slide of his microscope. Then Wilson peaked into the lens. He saw that each snowflake had six sides.

_____ **a.** Wilson's mother gave him a microscope.

_____ **b.** Wilson was always looking into things.

B. Wilson raced back into the house. He begged his mother for a piece of black velvet cloth. Then he raced back outside. Next, he tried to catch snowflakes on the velvet. More and more flakes fell onto the dark cloth. When Wilson looked at them, he saw that each snowflake had a different design. For the next two years, Wilson tried to draw the pretty designs. He had two problems. He was not very good at drawing. The snowflakes melted too quickly.

_____ **a.** Wilson tried to draw the pretty designs.

_____ **b.** Wilson saw that each snowflake had a different design.

C. Wilson's family thought of a way to solve his problems. They saved their money all year. They bought him a special camera. It could take pictures through a microscope. For two years Wilson Bentley tried to get just the pictures he wanted. He had no luck. People in Jericho thought he was just plain crazy. Then, on January 15, 1885, five inches of snow fell. During the storm, Wilson finally took a picture of a snowflake.

For forty years, Bentley took pictures of snowflakes. He studied snowflakes, too. He learned more about snowflakes than anyone else in the world. People began to call him "The Snowflake Man."

_____ **a.** In 1885, Wilson took the first picture of a snowflake.

_____ **b.** Wilson's family bought him a special camera.

_____ **c.** Wilson had no luck taking pictures of snowflakes.

D. Bentley's pictures became famous. Many people bought them. Then they copied the snowflake designs. They used the designs for jewelry and wallpaper. People wanted to hear how he had taught himself to take better snowflake pictures.

Bently became famous, but he never changed. He still used the camera he got when he was seventeen. He took almost six thousand pictures with it. Finally, when he was in his sixties, one of his books was published. It was all about the snowflakes he loved so much. No one thought he was crazy any more. They said that Bentley, like each of his beloved snowflakes, was one of a kind.

_____ **a.** Then people copied his snowflake designs.

_____ **b.** Bentley's book about snowflakes was published.

_____ **c.** People bought Bentley's pictures.

REMEMBER Sequence is the order in which things happen.

The Life of an Island

Miles below the surface the ocean floor starts to shake. Sand floats up. Fish feel the water moving as they swim. Then a large crack opens in the bottom of the ocean. An island is about to be born. In this lesson, you will learn that an island, like a person, changes throughout its lifetime. You will also learn about sequence.

1 KEYS to Sequence

Events in a story happen in sequence.

LEARN The events in a story happen in a certain order, or sequence. Knowing the sequence can help you understand why things happen.

DIRECTIONS Read the words and phrases in the box. Use them to help you underline the word or phrase in each sentence that gives a clue to the sequence of events.

at first	next	then	after	finally	again	at last

1. The ocean floor shakes lightly at first.
2. Again the floor shakes.
3. Then the sand moves and settles back down.
4. Finally a crack appears in the ocean floor.
5. Next hot melted rock called lava flows through the crack.
6. After the sea floor cracks, tons of lava from inside the earth pile up.
7. At last the tip of the mountain breaks through the water.
8. An island has finally been born.

DIRECTIONS Read each pair of sentences. Use clue words to help you decide what the correct sequence should be. Then circle the letter of the sentence that tells what happened first.

1. **a.** Then, one day, the volcano settles down.
   b. Months pass, and the volcano keeps on growing.
2. **a.** Thousands of tiny animals called coral are floating in the water around the island.
   b. The coral begin to settle onto the sides of the island.
3. **a.** Waves crash against the volcano.
   b. Finally the hard lava starts to crack and crumble and turn into soil.
4. **a.** Next the seeds sprout and begin to grow.
   b. Tiny seeds blow in from far away and drop into a crack in the soil.
5. **a.** Then other living things ride to the island on the feathers and feet of sea birds.
   b. The wind sprinkles the island with spiders and insects.
6. **a.** All kinds of seeds wash up on the shore of the volcano.
   b. Finally, over many more years, the island is covered with green plants.

3 Read and Apply

DIRECTIONS Read the paragraphs. Number the events to show the correct sequence.

1. One day something special comes to the island. It is a clump of floating trees, vines, roots, and weeds. The plants are from an island far away. They were carried out to sea. At last they wash up onto a beach on the island. A fat green lizard crawls off the raft. Then she lays her eggs on the island. Finally the eggs hatch and the island has a whole family of lizards.

_____ **a.** The lizard eggs hatch.

_____ **b.** Trees, vines, roots, and weeds are carried out to sea.

_____ **c.** The plants wash up onto a beach on the new island.

_____ **d.** A fat green lizard crawls onto the island.

2. Many years later a ship stops near the island. Then some scientists row up to the island in small boats. They have come to study the animals. Before they go, something new is added to the island. Now there are a few rats. The rats were hiding in some boxes the scientists brought with them. They now have a new home.

_____ **a.** The scientists row small boats up to the island.

_____ **b.** When the scientists leave, rats remain on the island.

_____ **c.** A ship stops near the island.

_____ **d.** The scientists study animals on the island.

The huge volcano island is very heavy. From the beginning, it has been sinking into the ocean. Year after year, rain and crashing waves beat at the island. It wears down. It grows smaller and smaller. Plants and animals start to die out.

Tiny animals called coral live in the sea around the island. They build stony skeletons around themselves. The skeletons grow together. The collection of skeletons becomes a coral reef. After many years, the reef forms a ring around the island. At last, fish and other sea life move in. They make the reef their home.

Meanwhile, the volcano sinks deeper every year. In about twenty million years, it sinks back under the sea. Finally, the island is gone. In the end, only the coral reef is left.

One day, the ocean floor begins to shake again. At first, it shakes lightly. Then it shakes harder and harder. It starts to crack. Can you guess what is going to happen?

1. Rain and waves wear down the island ____ it sinks.
   a. before
   b. after
   c. next

2. A ring of coral grows ____ the island is formed.
   a. first
   b. before
   c. after

3. In about twenty million years, the island ____ disappears.
   a. last
   b. after
   c. finally

4. One day, the ocean floor begins to shake ____.
   a. then
   b. again
   c. after

REMEMBER Sequence can help you understand why things happen.

Backyard Wildlife Refuge

Do you know you are a detective every time you read? Whenever you read, you search for clues. Some clues are in the words you read. Other clues are "between the lines" or in your head. In this lesson, you will read about helping wild animals. You will learn to read between the lines.

1 KEYS to Making Inferences

Use your head to understand what you read.

LEARN You make inferences every day. If you see snow on the ground, you infer that you need warm clothes. You also make inferences when you read. Some clues are already stored in your head, just waiting for you to use them. When you read the words, what you already know can help you.

DIRECTIONS Read the paragraph. Then read the questions below it. Don't answer the questions. Instead write P on the line if the words are right on the page. Write H if you have to use your head.

You can build a wildlife refuge in your own backyard. It doesn't take much space. With a little planning and work, you can attract birds, mammals, reptiles, and insects. The refuge will help wildlife. Your family will enjoy it, too.

_____ **1.** Is a wildlife refuge a safe place for animals?

_____ **2.** Will birds come to your refuge?

_____ **3.** Will your refuge help wildlife?

DIRECTIONS Read the story. Use the words on the page and the ideas in your head to answer the questions.

When fall came, Jean worried about the animals. She wondered how to help them. Then she had an idea. She would turn the yard into a wildlife refuge. She hoped squirrels, rabbits, chipmunks, and other animals would soon make their homes in her backyard.

Planning safe hiding places for animals took time. First she piled branches and twigs under a large tree. Then she gathered stones and piled them near some low bushes.

Once the shelters were built, Jean worked on water and food supplies. She turned a lid from an old garbage can upside down and put it near the shelters. She would fill it every day.

Tablescraps would be one source of food. To give her animal friends a good diet, she collected nuts and seeds. She picked wild berries and dried them on the windowsill in the garage. She spent her allowance on a large sack of shelled corn.

Now all Jean had to do was sit back and wait for the animals to find their new home.

1. What will the garbage can lid be used for?

_____

_____

_____

2. Why didn't Jean dry the berries outside?

_____

_____

_____

3. What animals might make their homes in the woodpile?

_____

_____

_____

3   Read and Apply

DIRECTIONS Maybe you would rather attract birds than animals. Tell what you already know about birds. Read the article. Answer the questions.

Planning a wildlife refuge for birds takes some work. Birds need places to rest where they will be hidden from their enemies. You might need to plant some bushes. It's a good idea to add a few birdhouses.

Birds build nests in different shapes and sizes. They may build their nests from sticks, grass, feathers, hair, ribbons, yarn, bark, leaves, straw, moss, and many other things. Collect a variety of scraps and place them outdoors. The birds will find them.

1. Where do birds rest, eat, and sleep?

   _____

   _____

   _____

2. What do birds use to build their nests?

   _____

   _____

   _____

3. What do birds eat and drink?

   _____

   _____

   _____

Birds need water and food to stay alive and healthy. Berries and nuts are one type of nourishing food. Sunflowers attract seed-eating birds. Insects found in tree bark, among dead leaves, or in the ground are another source of food. Dry bread or unsalted peanuts are real treats. You can buy birdseed for a birdfeeder.

Add water and you will have a good bird refuge. Remember that birds will come to depend on your refuge for food. Be sure to check your birdfeeder and refill your water source every day.

DIRECTIONS Read the sentences. Then write each sentence under the correct heading to tell whether you read the information right on the page or used what you already knew to read between the lines.

1. Birds need water and food to stay alive and healthy.

2. Stale crackers would attract birds.

3. It might take several weeks to make a bird refuge.

4. Birds build nests in different shapes and sizes.

5. Birds will find nest materials you leave outside.

6. Planting a berry bush would help attract birds.

On the Page

_____

_____

_____

_____

_____

Between the Lines

_____

_____

_____

_____

_____

_____

REMEMBER Use your head to understand your reading.

The History of Marshmallows

It's fun to play guessing games. Do you know you play a guessing game every time you read?

In this lesson, you will read about marshmallows. You will practice making good guesses.

1 KEYS to Making Inferences

An inference is a good guess.

LEARN When you read, the words on the page can't tell you everything. Sometimes you need to use the words on the page with ideas already in your head to make a guess. Making good guesses while you read is called making inferences.

DIRECTIONS Read the paragraph. Then read the ideas. Circle the numbers of the clues that you found in the paragraph. Underline the numbers of the clues you had to guess.

Years ago, cave people used many plants to make medicines. One plant was used to make a syrup for coughs. It was used for sore throats, too. The same plant made a salve for sores or burns. That plant was called a marshmallow.

1. Cave people used plants to make medicines.
2. Cave people were glad whenever they found a marshmallow.
3. Without marshmallows cave people would be sick more often.
4. Marshmallow is the name of a plant.

Practice Making Inferences

DIRECTIONS Read each paragraph and the statements below it. Write I on the line before the statement if you had to make an inference. Write P if the statement is right on the page.

A. Marshmallow plants grew wild in Europe. They were found in marshes along the coast. When the first settlers came to North America, they brought the seeds of the marshmallow plant with them. The seeds dropped to the ground. They began growing. Soon marshes along the coastline of North America had many marshmallow plants.

_____ **1.** The marshes in Europe are like marshes in North America.

_____ **2.** Marshmallow plants grew wild in Europe.

_____ **3.** Marshmallows came to North America with European settlers.

B. A marshmallow plant grows very tall. Its leaves are a soft grayish-green. Beautiful pink or lavender flowers, about the size of a quarter, bloom on the plant late each summer. The long white root of the marshmallow looks something like a carrot. The root is the part of the plant that was used to make medicine.

_____ **1.** You won't find marshmallow flowers in May.

_____ **2.** The flowers are not useful for making medicine.

_____ **3.** A marshmallow plant is tall.

Read and Apply

DIRECTIONS Read the story about marshmallows. Answer the questions on the next page. Some of the answers will be right in the story. You will need to make inferences to answer others.

One day, somewhere, a person stood over a fire stirring a thick batch of marshmallow root. Suddenly an idea flashed into the stirrer's mind. The marshmallow mixture looked and smelled so good. What would happen if a little sugar were added? Into the pot went the sugar! Now the marshmallow root not only looked good and smelled good. It also tasted delicious. The first marshmallow candy had been invented.

Today there are many marshmallow products in the store. You can buy large or small marshmallows in bags. Some people like to roast the large ones over a campfire. The small ones are used in salads or for decorating cookies. Marshmallow sauce goes on ice cream sundaes. Marshmallows can be found in candy, cookies, salads, and cereals.

The settlers who brought the first marshmallows to the North American coast would not recognize today's marshmallows. Today's marshmallows taste good. They are not at all like medicine, though. Marshmallow roots are no longer used to make them. They are made from sugar, starch, syrup, and other ingredients.

DIRECTIONS Write T on the line if the statement is true. Write F if it is false.

_____ 1. We know the name of the person who invented marshmallow candy.

_____ 2. Before sugar was added, the marshmallow root mixture probably didn't taste very good.

_____ 3. Before sugar was added, the marshmallow root mixture probably didn't smell or look good.

_____ 4. Today there are many products made with marshmallow roots.

_____ 5. Some cookies have marshmallows in them.

_____ 6. The settlers who brought marshmallows to North America would recognize today's marshmallows.

_____ 7. Most people think today's marshmallows taste like medicine.

_____ 8. Today's marshmallows are healthier to eat than the marshmallow root.

_____ 9. Today's marshmallows contain sugar.

_____ 10. If you take cough medicine, it is probably made of marshmallows.

REMEMBER Use the words on the page and the clues in your head.

Do Monsters Exist?

Some scientists keep busy by checking into reports of strange animals. Some people call these strange animals "monsters."

In this lesson, you will learn what scientists think about monsters. You will learn the difference between facts and opinions.

 ## KEYS to Fact and Opinion

Facts can be checked. Opinions are what we think.

LEARN A fact tells about something that has happened or something that is true. We can prove that a fact is true or false.

An opinion tells how someone feels or what someone thinks may happen. Some words are clues to opinions. Some of these clue words are: *think, believe, seem, might, could,* and *feel.*

EXAMPLE Fact: Another name for Bigfoot is Sasquatch.
Opinion: I think Bigfoot is a large ape.

DIRECTIONS Read each statement. Circle F if the statement is a fact and can be proven. Circle O if the statement is an opinion.

1. A man in Washington pretended to be Bigfoot.   F   O

2. He used fake feet to make fake footprints.   F   O

3. The pictures of Bigfoot might be fake, too.   F   O

4. We think Bigfoot might really exist.   F   O

5. Most scientists feel that more proof is needed.   F   O

2 Practice With Fact and Opinion

DIRECTIONS Read the story. Find the number in front of each sentence. Write the numbers of the facts on the lines.

(1)A man in Texas thinks he saw a monster. (2)It flew over the bus he was driving. (3)The animal was covered with thick hide. (4)Its tail was shaped like a fin. (5)It had a bump on its head.

(6)Three teachers also reported seeing these strange animals. (7)The animals were flying above some cows. (8)A Texas naturalist does not believe these animals were monsters. (9)He thinks they are glider airplanes. (10)They may also be low-flying sea birds.

Facts: _____ _____ _____ _____ _____ _____

DIRECTIONS Now read about Wildman. This time write the numbers of the opinion sentences.

(1)People in China have reported seeing a creature called Wildman. (2)They think Wildman may be a monster. (3)Wildman is about five feet tall. (4)He is covered with reddish hair. (5)Some people believe Wildman can smile and cry.

(6)Scientists think they have found samples of Wildman's hair.

(7)Some of the hair is the same as the hair of a rare kind of monkey. (8)Casts have been made of Wildman's footprints. (9)The footprints seem to belong to a large monkey. (10)A few scientists feel that Wildman may be a large ape.

Opinions: _____ _____ _____ _____ _____

82 Fact and Opinion

DIRECTIONS Read about a monster that suddenly appeared one morning on a Florida beach. Which statements are facts? Which are opinion?

Many years ago, in 1896, a giant creature washed up on a beach in Florida. Early morning fishermen were surprised to find its massive hulk on the beach. Some fishermen refused to go near the monster. They were afraid it could hurt them. Those fishermen ran away from the beach.

Word about the monster spread quickly. Soon the beach was filled with curious people. The people gave the creature a name. They called it the Florida Monster.

Later that morning, scientists arrived at the scene. They tried to figure out what the huge beast could be. Some scientists thought it was a small whale. Others thought it was a very large squid. One scientist took a sample of the creature's skin. He preserved it in a bottle.

Years passed. Most people who had seen the Florida Monster were dead. The Florida Monster was almost forgotten. Then, one day, another scientist came across the preserved skin. He found out all he could about the monster. Science had come a long way since 1896, he thought. Could he solve the mystery after all this time?

The scientist used modern equipment and new knowledge about sea creatures. He tested the sample of preserved skin. The skin was not like a whale's skin. It was not like the skin of a squid. What do you think the strange animal really was? Was it a monster? The scientist doesn't think so. He thinks the Florida Monster was nothing more than an extra-large octopus.

DIRECTIONS Find three facts and three opinions in the story. Write them on the correct lines.

Facts

1. _____

_____

2. _____

_____

3. _____

_____

Opinions

1. _____

_____

2. _____

_____

3. _____

_____

REMEMBER Facts can be checked. Opinions are thoughts.

Chicken Nuggets

Chickens are probably the best known birds in the world. Millions of chickens are raised each year. In this lesson, you will learn about fact and opinion as you read about chickens.

 ## 1 KEYS to Fact and Opinion

Facts can be proved. Opinions are thoughts or feelings.

LEARN A fact tells something that can be checked. Here is fact: Chickens lay eggs. It is a fact because we can check to see if it is true.

An opinion tells how we feel or what we think. Here is an opinion: Tony's brother thinks chickens make good pets. It is an opinion because it tells what someone thinks. Words like *think, believe,* or *seem* are clues that a statement is an opinion.

DIRECTIONS Read each sentence. Put an X in the correct column to show whether it is a fact or an opinion.

	Fact	Opinion
1. Chickens eat corn.	____	____
2. Chickens seem to be good pets.	____	____
3. A chicken lays about 250 eggs a year.	____	____
4. Some people say chicken soup cures a cold.	____	____
5. Many people think chicken is good to eat.	____	____

DIRECTIONS Read each pair of sentences. In each pair, one sentence is a fact and the other is an opinion. Write F beside each fact. Write O beside each opinion.

1. _____ **a.** Many people eat chicken for dinner.

_____ **b.** My friend thinks chicken is the best food ever.

2. _____ **a.** My dad believes eggs with white shells taste better than eggs with brown shells.

_____ **b.** Chickens may lay white or brown eggs.

3. _____ **a.** Sometimes chickens eat things that make them sick.

_____ **b.** I think chickens eat everything they see.

4. _____ **a.** You can have white meat or dark meat when you eat chicken.

_____ **b.** Some people think white meat tastes better than dark meat.

5. _____ **a.** The Chinese believed a chicken would protect the mother of a family when the father was away.

_____ **b.** In some countries, chickens live in the house with the family.

3 | Read and Apply

DIRECTIONS Read about some rare chickens. Write two sentences from the story that are facts. Write two more that are opinions.

1There are more than 150 different kinds of chickens. **2**Some are very small. **3**Other chickens seem to be giants.

4Some people, known as chicken fanciers, make a hobby of raising chickens. **5**They do not raise chickens for eggs or meat. **6**They think a chicken's looks are more important than its taste.

7Chicken fanciers enter their chickens in contests. **8**Many contestants seem to be dressed in funny costumes. **9**Some have feathers that stand up high on their heads. **10**Others have feathers that

look like long ears. **11**Some chickens have tails almost as long as a school bus. **12**I believe these are the funniest chickens of all.

Facts

1. _____

   _____

2. _____

   _____

Opinions

1. _____

   _____

2. _____

   _____

People in India and China began raising chickens about 5,000 years ago. The people of India thought chickens were special. They had a law against eating them.

The people of Greece raised some of their chickens for chicken fights. They raised other chickens for their eggs. The Greeks believed the chickens made good alarm clocks.

In Rome, people used chickens to predict what would happen in the future. The chickens were fed just before the men went into battle. If the chickens ate well, the Romans believed their men would win.

Some people think soldiers from Spain brought the first chickens to North America. Later, when the Pilgrims came, they kept chickens for eating. The Pilgrims also raised chickens for their eggs.

REMEMBER Facts can be proved. Opinions cannot.

Spider Tales

Maybe you know someone who doesn't like spiders. To some people spiders mean good luck. In the lesson, you will read interesting facts about spiders. You will learn about cause and effect.

 ## 1 KEYS to Cause and Effect

Why did it happen?

LEARN The reason something happens is called the cause. The thing that happens is the effect. The cause makes the effect happen. Follow the steps to find the cause and effect.

The spider spun a web because it wanted to trap food.

> Step 1: Ask, "What happened?" The answer to this question (The spider spun a web) is the effect.
>
> Step 2: Ask, "Why did it happen?" The answer to this question (because it wanted to trap food) is the cause.

DIRECTIONS Read each sentence. Is the underlined part the cause or the effect? If it is the cause, circle C. If it is the effect, circle E.

1. Some people feel strange because a spider is near.   C   E

2. Since spiders eat harmful insects, farmers like to see them at harvest time.   C   E

3. Some spiders make little silk pads in the middle of their webs, so they will have a place to sit.   C   E

DIRECTIONS Read each sentence. Decide which part is the cause and which part is the effect. Draw one line under the cause. Draw two lines under the effect. The first one is done for you.

1. Some Spiders are called web spinners, because they spin webs to catch food.

2. Since it takes only about an hour to make a web, some spiders spin a new web every night.

3. Since spiders webs are sticky, flies get caught in them.

4. Because garden spiders do not see well, they depend on the movement of the web to let them know they have caught some food.

5. Spiders often let wasps and bees get out of their webs, because they do not want to be stung.

6. Many people do not destroy spider webs, since the webs are so beautiful.

Read and Apply

DIRECTIONS Read the story to learn how people felt about spiders long ago. Think about cause and effect as you read.

When you were younger, you probably learned the nursery rhyme "Little Miss Muffet." Did you know there really was a Little Miss Muffet? She lived in the 1500s. Her father was a doctor who had some strange ideas about medicine.

Dr. Muffet thought keeping spiders in the house would keep his family healthy. He let spiders spin webs all over the house. He never let anyone tear a spider web down. When Little Miss Muffet did get sick, her father would give her pills made from spiders.

Many years ago people believed that spiders could cure illness. Because they thought spiders were healthy, doctors gave spider medicine to their patients.

While Dr. Muffet was growing spiders in his home, another doctor had some different ideas about spider medicine. This doctor had an interesting cure for fevers. If his patient had a fever, the doctor prescribed spider and butter sandwiches. He also told his patients to eat spiders wrapped in raisins to get well.

Other doctors thought spider webs were better medicine than spiders. To cure a fever, these doctors mixed spider webs with frog legs. They also liked to put spider webs on cuts to make bleeding stop.

A good cure is important, but it would be even better not to get sick in the first place. Many people in the 1500s thought having a spider with them would keep

them from getting sick. That is why they carried spiders with them at all times. They kept the spiders in tiny, specially-made boxes or nutshells.

Before your next trip to the doctor's office, imagine for a minute that you lived in the 1500s. Aren't you glad you live now? Wouldn't you rather have a shot than a spider and butter sandwich?

DIRECTIONS Finish each sentence by writing the cause on the line

so they would not get sick.
so the bleeding would stop.
because he thought they could cure fevers.
because her father was famous for spider medicine.
because he thought spiders would keep his family healthy.

1. The nursery rhyme about Miss Muffet was probably written

_____

_____

2. Dr. Muffet let spiders spin webs in his house

_____

_____

3. People carried boxes and shells containing spiders

_____

_____

4. One doctor prescribed spider and butter sandwiches

_____

_____

5. Spider webs were placed on cuts

_____

_____

REMEMBER The cause tells why the effect happens.

Eagle Feathers

Have you ever heard someone use the expression "a feather in my cap"? In this lesson you will read about how this expression came to be. You will learn about cause and effect.

 1 ## KEYS to Cause and Effect

Cause and effect go together.

LEARN When something happens, it often makes something else happen. This is called cause and effect. When you know what happened, you know the effect. When you know why it happened, you know the cause.

EXAMPLE Native Americans did a special dance because they wanted rain.

The words "because they wanted rain" tell us why the Native Americans danced. This is the cause. The words "Native Americans did a special dance" tell what happened. This is the effect.

DIRECTIONS Draw one line under the cause in each sentence. Draw two lines under the effect. The first one is done for you.

1. Native Americans planted corn so they could use it for food.

2. Since shells were so plentiful, they were used for tools.

3. Native American Indians collected eagle feathers because the feathers meant good luck.

2 Practice With Cause and Effect

DIRECTIONS Read the causes and effects. Match each cause with its effect by writing the letter of the cause on the line. The first one is done for you.

Effect   Cause

_C_ **1.** They built canoes   **A.** so they can learn.

____ **2.** They made belts from   **B.** because they wanted to scare
beads   evil spirits away.

____ **3.** He dried his bike   **C.** so they could travel on water.

____ **4.** They saved the skins   **D.** because she wore her raincoat.
from deer

____ **5.** They wore masks   **E.** to correct any errors.

____ **6.** She did not get wet   **F.** because they used them to
trade for things they needed.

____ **7.** She rewrote her paper   **G.** because they could make warm
clothes from them.

____ **8.** Children go to school   **H.** so it wouldn't rust.

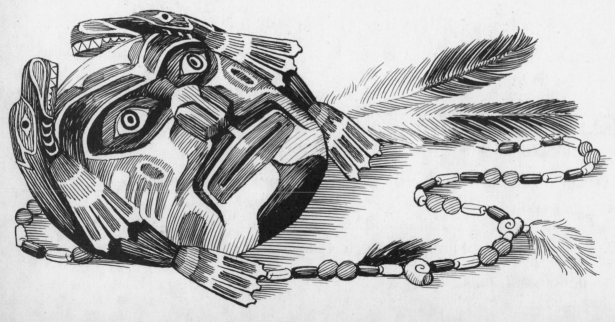

DIRECTIONS Read the story. Think about why things happened.

When you are praised for something you have done, we say you have "a feather in your cap." If you do many good deeds, you will have many feathers in your cap.

This expression came to be used because Native American Indians earned an eagle's tail feather for each brave deed they did. They wore the feathers in their hair.

A warrior who did many brave deeds would make a beautiful headdress from his many feathers. When he wore the bonnet of beautiful feathers, other people would show respect.

The treasured eagle feathers were used in many other ways. Native Americans sewed the feathers on their clothes and used them to decorate spears and shields. They wanted to show that they were strong and brave like eagles.

Eagle feathers were used for "snake whips" by some tribes. Before using a snake in a rain dance, they touched the snake with an eagle feather. Because the feather had touched it, they believed, the snake would behave.

It would not bite anyone.

Some modern Native Americans still like to keep a supply of eagle feathers. They still use the feathers for many things. The feathers are harder to get today. Eagles are an endangered species. There are laws against hunting eagles.

The United States government helps both the eagles and the Native Americans. It saves the feathers from eagles who die by accident or are killed illegally. Native Americans can have the feathers whenever they need them.

Cause and Effect **95**

1. You get a "feather in your cap,"

_____

_____

2. _____

_____

_____ to get respect from other Native Americans.

3. The United States government saves eagle feathers

_____

_____

_____

4. _____

_____ because they are an endangered species.

5. _____

_____

_____ so the snake would behave and not bite.

6. Native Americans decorated spears and shields with eagle feathers

_____

_____

_____

_____

7. A warrior earned many feathers

_____

_____

REMEMBER The cause tells why the effect happened.

Using Your Mind

Did you know your mind has to work hard to learn something new? Your mind compares a new idea to ideas it has already learned and stored away. That's a tough job. In this lesson, you will give your mind practice by making comparisons.

---

 1 ## KEYS to Comparing

Comparing is deciding how things are alike or different.

LEARN When you compare, you tell how things are alike. You also tell how they are different.

DIRECTIONS Complete the story by filling in the blanks. There are many possible answers. Compare your story with a friend's story.

When I was young, dogs and cats probably looked alike to me. They both

had _____, _____, _____, and _____.
I probably thought they were both the same animal.

As I grew older, I realized they were very different. I noticed that a cat

says, _____, and a dog says, _____. Many cats' ears are

_____, but dogs' ears are _____. Cats like to

_____, but dogs like to _____.

2 Practice Making Comparisons

DIRECTIONS Make comparisons by using the words in the box to complete each sentence. Use each word only once.

sticky	daisy	wiggly	juicy	shiny	liquids	glass
bluish	rough	bendable	tall	heavy	clouds	

1. Wire and rubber are

   _____, while

   _____ is not.

2. Stars and aluminum foil are

   _____.

3. Sandpaper and a cat's tongue

   are _____.

4. Bricks and cars are

   _____, but feathers
   are not.

5. Water is not _____,
   but glue and gum are.

6. Trees and telephone poles are

   _____, but a

   _____ is not.

7. Rain and soda pop are

   _____, but carpets
   are not.

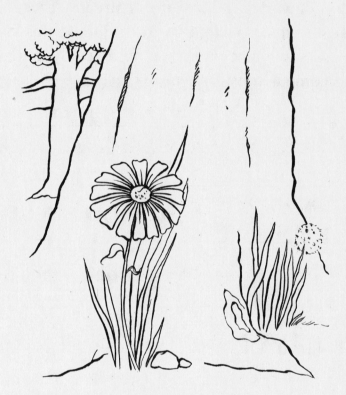

8. A banana is not

   _____, though an
   orange is.

9. The sea and sky are

   _____, but

   _____ are not.

10. Jello and cooked noodles are

    _____.

Read and Apply

DIRECTIONS When things change, you can compare the way they used to be with the way they are now. Read the poem about how people change.

I'm Changing

When I was young,
Just three or four,
I couldn't reach
Much off the floor.

By five or six,
Life was a charm,
I'd reach most things,
Stretching my arm.

Seven years passed.
I grew so strong.
The eighth year came.
My legs were long.

This year I'm nine,
Soon I'll be ten.
Can you guess what?
I've grown again.

—Sandra Dahl

DIRECTIONS Compare yourself to the child you used to be. Think back. List your favorites when you were in first grade. List your favorites now. How have you changed? How have you stayed the same?

Favorite	First Grade	Now
1. Food		
2. TV Show		
3. Game		
4. Sport		
5. Toy		
6. Song		
7. Book		
8. School Subject		
9. Place to Go		
10. Friend		
11. Shoe Size		
12. Hero		
13. Height		
14. Talent		

REMEMBER You learn by comparing.

People Are Different

How are you and your best friend alike? How are you different? In this lesson, you will learn to compare and contrast to find out how people and things are alike and different.

KEYS to Comparing

Compare = alike.   Contrast = different.

LEARN When you tell how two or more things are the same, you are comparing them. When you tell how they differ, you contrast them.

EXAMPLE Compare and contrast a bicycle and a skateboard.

Compare: Both have wheels.
Contrast: A bicycle has pedals,
but a skateboard doesn't.

DIRECTIONS Compare or contrast. Write one sentence for each item.

1. Compare a sofa and a chair. _____

_____

2. Compare a radio and a TV. _____

_____

3. Contrast a pen and a pencil. _____

_____

4. Contrast a pond and an ocean. _____

_____

Practice Comparing and Contrasting

DIRECTIONS Read about Erin and Missy. Use the information to write sentences to compare and contrast them. The first one in each section has been done for you.

Erin

. . .lives in Carmel, California.
. . .likes to ride horses.
. . .walks to school.
. . .loves to read mysteries.
. . .plays soccer.
. . .speaks English.

Missy

. . .plays softball and soccer.
. . .loves animal stories.
. . .speaks Spanish and English.
. . .takes ballet lessons.
. . .rides a bus to school.
. . .lives in Woodside, California.

Compare

1. Erin and Missy both live in California.

2. _____

3. _____

4. _____

Contrast

1. Erin lives in Carmel, but Missy lives in Woodside.

2. _____

3. _____

4. _____

DIRECTIONS What if all people and things in the world were alike? Read the story to find out.

Arnie slammed the door. He threw his books down. His dog, Bouncer, raced to meet him, but Arnie walked right by.

Dad looked up from his newspaper. "You don't seem to be in a very good mood," he said.

"I'm mad at Ronnie," Arnie said. "I wanted to work on our models after school. He doesn't want to. He doesn't like anything I like anymore. When we were little, we did everything together. Now he's different. I wish Ronnie were just like me."

"That would really be boring," said Dad. "It's good that people and things are different. That makes life interesting."

"Parents!" thought Arnie disgustedly. He was bored. He looked at his model. It reminded him he was mad at Ronnie. He felt so bad he decided to go to bed.

Arnie heard a knock at the door. "It's Ronnie," a voice called.

When Arnie opened the door, he thought he was looking in the

mirror. There stood a boy who looked just like him.

"Your wish came true," Ronnie said. "We are just alike. I want to do just what you do."

"Oh, boy," thought Arnie, and they went up to build models. Soon they both got tired of models. They both spoke at the same time. They decided to ride their bikes to Ronnie's house.

Out on the street, Arnie got another surprise. Other boys were playing outside. They all looked just like Ronnie and Arnie. They were all dressed alike. They were riding their bikes, too.

Arnie looked around some more. Every house looked just alike. Each one had a dog in the yard. They all looked just like Bouncer.

As the day wore on, Arnie got more and more bored. Talking to Ronnie was just like talking to himself. Everything and everyone looked just the same. All his friends had the same games.

"This is a nightmare," said Arnie. "Dad was right. The world is boring when everything is the same. I wish things were the way they were."

Arnie heard another knock on his door. He sat up. He was in his bed.

"Ronnie's on the phone," Dad called.

Arnie smiled. Ronnie wasn't angry. Arnie wouldn't be angry either. He was glad Ronnie was different. Before he went to the phone, Arnie did one thing. He looked out the bedroom window. He was glad to see that each house on his street was different.

DIRECTIONS Read each sentence. Write the number of each sentence on the correct line.

1. Wanda lives in a house, but Andy lives in an apartment.
2. They are both friends of mine.
3. The number 8 is even, while 5 is odd.
4. Mike helped us, and so did Lauren.
5. Eggs, cereal, and waffles are breakfast foods.
6. A story is usually longer than a poem.

Comparisons _____ _____ _____
Contrasts _____ _____ _____

REMEMBER Compare and contrast to find likenesses and differences.

Think Fast!

Can you remember a time when you had to think and act quickly? In this lesson, you will read about a family that had to act quickly when they spotted a tornado. You will learn about words that do not always mean what they say.

 KEYS to Figures of Speech

Figures of speech paint pictures in your mind.

LEARN Authors sometimes use words in ways that give them special meanings. These words do not mean exactly what they say. They help you see a picture in your mind. These words are called figures of speech.

EXAMPLE Tim and I saw the storm coming toward us. We ran for the house. We were lucky. We made it just under the wire.

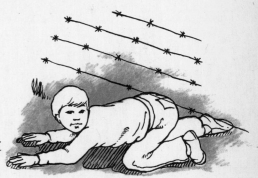

The words *just under the wire* do not mean that Tim and I had to crawl under a wire to get inside. They mean that Tim and I got inside the house just before the rain came.

DIRECTIONS Underline the figure of speech in each sentence. Write the real meaning of the underlined words on the line.

1. It was raining cats and dogs.

_____

2. A storm like that happens once in a blue moon.

_____

Practice With Figures of Speech

(2)

DIRECTIONS Read the sentences. The underlined words are figures of speech. Choose the best meaning for each figure of speech. Write its letter in the space above the number of the sentence. The correct answers will spell out what the figures of speech have in common. The first one has been done for you.

1. Sometimes my big brother really <u>gets my goat</u>.

   n. a hoarse voice

2. Katie couldn't sing because she had <u>a frog in her throat</u>.

   l. was crazy

3. I wanted to keep Dad's present a surprise but Barbara <u>let the cat out of the bag</u>.

   A. makes me angry

4. Mom called the ugly old lamp <u>a white elephant</u> and threw it in the trash.

   s. largest amount

5. If you think Eddie will do your chores, you're <u>barking up the wrong tree</u>.

   m. an unwanted object

6. When I told Grandpa I had seen a flying saucer, he said I <u>had bats in my belfry</u>.

   i. told the secret

7. Both girls were supposed to clean the room, but Emily did the <u>lion's share</u> of the job.

   a. making a mistake

$$\underline{\quad A \quad} \ \underline{\qquad} \ \underline{\qquad} \ \underline{\qquad} \ \underline{\qquad} \ \underline{\qquad} \ \underline{\qquad}$$
$$\ \ 1 \qquad 2 \qquad 3 \qquad 4 \qquad 5 \qquad 6 \qquad 7$$

Read and Apply

DIRECTIONS Read about a family who remained safe because they knew tornado safety rules. Circle the correct meaning of each underlined figure of speech.

One boring June afternoon suddenly became a (**1**) red-letter day. I'll never forget it. My sister and I were outside (**2**) minding our P's and Q's. Then Dad came out. He pointed to the sky. (**3**) My heart stood still when I saw the green-black cloud. A tornado was moving toward us (**4**) like a house afire.

Nancy and I remembered what we had learned during Tornado Safety Week. We (**5**) flew down the basement stairs and crawled under a table in the southwest corner. That way, if our house blew down, (**6**) the whole kit and caboodle wouldn't fall on us.

1. birthday

   Valentine's Day

   important day

2. playing with alphabet blocks

   doing what we should

   eating alphabet soup

3. I was scared.

   My heart stopped beating.

   I was happy.

4. very slowly

   very quickly

   in flames

5. hurried

   flapped our wings

   slid

6. a few things

   a small piece

   the whole thing

Finish the story. Then underline the figures of speech. Write them on the lines.

The storm was over in a few minutes. Luckily, the tornado had leapfrogged over our house. Then we looked next door at Uncle Ray's place. His house was still standing, but his garage was a horse of a different color.

Uncle Ray had been working hard to fix up an old car. Some people thought his car was a lemon, but that car was the apple of his eye. He wanted to drive it in the Fourth of July parade.

Every Saturday he got up at the crack of dawn. He spent hours monkeying around under the hood. Now the car was covered with pieces of his garage.

I looked at Uncle Ray. He was down in the dumps. I offered to give him a hand. Uncle Ray started to smile. He was tickled pink by my offer.

We worked like beavers to clean up the mess. Now Uncle Ray can drive in the parade. Guess who will be right beside him.

1. _____

2. _____

3. _____

4. _____

5. _____

6. _____

7. _____

8. _____

9. _____

10. _____

REMEMBER Figures of speech make reading more fun.

Mind Power

The older you get, the more you have to remember. Your parents, your teachers, and even your friends all have something for you to remember. Sometimes you feel like your head will burst.

Don't give up! In this lesson, you will learn some tricks to help you memorize important things.

1 KEYS to Remembering

Concentrate! Organize! Review!

LEARN It's not hard to remember. Three steps will help you.

1. Concentrate: Put everything else out of your mind.
2. Organize: Group the information in a way that makes sense.
3. Review: Go over the information until you really know it.

DIRECTIONS Concentrate on the picture. Organize the items, or make up a story about what you see. After one minute, cover the picture. Write everything you remember on the lines. Then uncover the picture. How much did you remember?

_____

_____

_____

_____

Practice Remembering

DIRECTIONS Can you remember the three steps to memory power? Write them on the lines.

1. _____

2. _____

3. _____

DIRECTIONS Use the cartoon to help you answer the questions.

Look at the girl in the cartoon. Her name is Kathy. She has a problem. She has too many things to remember. Can you help her? Since we can only memorize one thing at a time, Kathy will concentrate on remembering her club meeting.

Step 1: Find the information about the meeting and concentrate on it. Read the information silently. Whisper it softly to yourself.

Step 2: Organize the information so it will be easy to remember. Kathy decided to organize the information by answering four important questions.

Step 3: Review the facts until you think you can remember them. Test yourself.

Cover the cartoon, and write the facts you remember. Then uncover the cartoon. Check your facts.

Who? _____

What? _____

When? _____

Where? _____

DIRECTIONS Learn a new trick for memorizing words in a list.

_____ _____

_____ _____

_____ _____

_____ _____

_____

Suppose you need to memorize the names of the planets in the solar system. Their names are Mercury, Venus, Earth, Mars, Jupiter, Saturn, Uranus, Neptune, and Pluto.

Study this sentence:

M̲y v̲ery e̲lderly m̲other j̲ust s̲erved u̲s n̲ine p̲izzas.

The first letter of each word is the same as the first letter of the name of a planet. The first letters are clues. The clues have been organized in a meaningful way.

Step 1: Concentrate on the list of planets.

Step 2: Learn the sentence.

Step 3: Cover the top of the page, and print the first letter of each word on a line. Beside each letter, write the name of a planet that starts with the same letter. (To name the planets in order from the sun, remember that _my_ ends with y, like Mercury.)

Make up your own memory aid. Suppose you need to remember a list of reptiles for a test. You have studied turtles, crocodiles, lizards, chameleons, alligators, and snakes. Follow the steps to make up your own trick.

1. Count the items in the list.

2. Print the first letter of each reptile's name on one of the lines.

___ ___ ___ ___ ___ ___

3. Group the letters so they make a word or phrase. The sillier it is, the easier it will be to remember.

Here is a phrase one person thought of: L. C. CATS. Make a picture in your mind. Someone named CATS might *be* a cat. Its name sounds like a business person's. L. C. CATS might carry a briefcase full of reptiles to remind you he is a memory aid for reptiles.

See if this silly phrase helped you remember the reptiles. Print the letters of L. C. Cats on the lines. Beside each letter, write the name of a reptile that begins with the same letter

_____ _____

_____ _____ _____

DIRECTIONS How well do you remember the information from this chapter? Answer the questions.

1. List the information about Kathy's meeting.

_____ _____

_____ _____

2. Name five things you remember from the picture.

_____ _____

_____ _____

_____

3. Name the plants in the solar system.

_____ _____

_____ _____

_____ _____

_____ _____

_____

4. Name six reptiles you studied in this lesson.

_____ _____

_____ _____

_____ _____

REMEMBER Use tricks to help you memorize.

_____

Seek and Find

When you know about indexes, you know a shortcut to finding the information you need. In this lesson, you will learn to use an index to find information in a hurry.

 ## KEYS to Using an Index

Look in the back of the book.

LEARN An index lists all the topics a book covers. You can find it in the back of the book. All books do not have indexes. A story book does not have an index. Most information books do.

The topics in an index are listed in alphabetical order. The page numbers tell you where to look. A dash between the numbers tells you there are several pages in a row about the topic.

DIRECTIONS Study the index. Use it to answer the questions.

Trap-door spider 107
Tree frog 195
Turkey 12, 46–47
Turtle 8, 23, 208–215

1. What topic would you find on page 195?

_____

2. How many pages tell about turtles?

_____

3. On which page would you read about trap-door spiders?

_____

4. Would this index be found in a story book or an information book?

_____

2 Practice With Indexes

DIRECTIONS Use the sample index from an animal encyclopedia to answer the questions.

Aardvark 80, 125
Ape 119, 345, 360
Bald eagle 113
Bat 13, 248, 367
Baltimore oriole 112
Bear 18, 24–25, 124
Beaver 13, 114–116
Bee 12, 62, 265
Bird 10, 101–105, 195, 201–205
Black-tailed deer 243
Bobcat 227
Camel 5
Cat 15, 20–32
Caterpillar 145–146

1. How many topics are listed in the index? _____

2. Where would you find information about bees? _____

3. What topic would you find on page 204? _____

4. What topics are listed between Bat and Beaver? _____
_____

5. Why is Camel listed before Cat and Caterpillar? _____
_____
_____

6. Which topic has the most pages?
_____

Read and Apply

3

DIRECTIONS An index can help when you have a report to write. Study the indexes. Answer the questions.

Animal Facts

Cape ground squirrel 528
Cape hunting dog 21, 180–81, 296
Caribou 16, 41, 120–125
Cat 126–137, 140–145
Cheetah 140–145
Chipmunk 152–153
Chimpanzee 146–151, 304

Wild Animals

Canada goose 64–67, 266
Carp 76
Cat 4–5, 290
Cattle 278
Chameleon 10
Chipmunk 307, 334–336
Cocoon 186
Coyote 162–165, 463

1. Which book has more pages about cats? _____

2. Which book has more pages about chipmunks? _____

3. Which topic has the most pages altogether? _____

4. Which pages would you use for a report on cats?

   Animal Facts: _____

   _____

   Wild Animals: _____

   _____

5. Which pages would you use for a report on chipmunks?

   Animal Facts: _____

   _____

   Wild Animals: _____

   _____

DIRECTIONS Use the cookbook
index to plan the menus below.
Write the correct page number
beside each recipe.

Animal pancakes 41
Apple juice delight 71
Applesauce cookies 32
Banana drink 11–12
Celery sticks 30
Cheese sandwich 33, 35
Chicken soup 25
Fruit salad 75
Green bean bake 28
Milk punch 12
Milk shake 13
Orange salad 83
Peanut butter sandwich 105
Pepperoni pizza 39
Sausage pizza 40
Snow ice cream 89
Tuna burger 22
Yogurt freeze 10–11

Menu 1

Peanut butter sandwich _____

Banana drink _____

Celery sticks _____

Menu 2

Animal pancakes _____

Apple juice delight _____

Menu 3

Pepperoni pizza _____

Fruit salad _____

Yogurt freeze _____

Menu 4

Cheese sandwich _____

Orange salad _____

Snow ice cream _____

Menu 5

Chicken soup _____

Green bean bake _____

Milk punch _____

Menu 6

Tuna burger _____

Milk shake _____

Applesauce cookies _____

REMEMBER Use the index to
find information fast.

Cat Patrol

You can't remember everything you read. It's hard enough to remember just the important things. First you have to decide just what the important things are. In this lesson, you will read about cats. You will learn to select important information.

 ## 1 KEYS to Selecting Information

What do you want to remember?

LEARN When you read for information, you must know why you are reading. Before you begin, ask yourself what question you want your book to answer. If you are reading a textbook, there may be questions at the end of the chapter. Study the questions before you begin to read.

DIRECTIONS Read to find out why your pet cat has claws and sharp teeth. Answer the questions.

Your pet cat is part of a much larger family. The cat family includes huge cats like lions and tigers, too. All cats are alike in many ways. To survive in the wild, cats must catch and eat other animals. Because wild cats must kill to survive, all cats have sharp claws and long, sharp teeth. When a cat kills, it is not being cruel. It is just using the survival instincts nature gave the whole cat family.

1. Why does a pet cat have claws and sharp teeth? _____

DIRECTIONS Sometimes you need to remember many details from one paragraph. Read the paragraph to remember what Siamese cats look like. Answer the questions.

The Siamese cat is one of the most popular short-haired cats. Many people think it is one of the most valuable cats. Siamese kittens are white when they are born. When they grow up, most Siamese cats change their color. They become tan or gray. Their faces, feet, ears, and tails are a darker shade. Most cats have yellow eyes, but Siamese cats have blue eyes. Some people think the blue eyes make the Siamese cat look more intelligent.

1. All Siamese cats have

   _____ hair.

2. Siamese kittens are born with

   _____ fur.

3. As they grow up, their fur turns

   _____ or

   _____ .

4. Their _____,

   _____,

   _____ , and

   _____ are a darker
   shade.

5. Siamese cats have

   _____ eyes.

DIRECTIONS Read to find out how cats are especially built to have keen senses. Answer the questions.

It's almost impossible to sneak up on a cat. That's because nature gave cats special equipment. They have very sharp senses.

Cats have yellow eyes. Their eyes have unusual pupils. They look like long, narrow slits. The slits act like window blinds. They let in just as much light as a cat needs. They open wide at night when there is not much light.

Cats have keen ears. The slightest noise will cause a cat to turn its head. Cats sleep lightly. Even in their sleep, they don't miss a thing. Cats can hear mice from as far away as twenty feet.

1. Circle the letter of the main idea of the article.

   a. Cats hear well.

   b. Cats have sharp senses.

   c. Cats can see at night.

2. What details did you learn about cats' senses?

   a. Sight: _____

   _____

   _____

   _____

   b. Hearing: _____

   _____

   _____

   _____

Some people think cats are unfriendly. Cat owners know better. Cats can be playful and gentle. Mother cats are especially tender. They take good care of their kittens.

Baby kittens are helpless when they are born. They cannot see because their eyes are not open. They cannot look for food. The mother cat feeds them milk. She protects them from danger. She cleans them with her rough tongue.

The mother cat does not let her kittens far from her sight. When a mother cat moves, she takes her kittens with her. She picks them up with her teeth by the loose skin on their necks. Cats have very sharp teeth, but a mother cat doesn't hurt her kittens. When she picks up her kittens, she is very gentle.

_____ 1. Mother cats prick their kittens with their sharp teeth.

_____ 2. Baby kittens cannot take care of themselves.

_____ 3. Kittens are born with their eyes closed.

_____ 4. Mother cats make their kittens get their own food.

_____ 5. Mother cats keep their babies near them.

_____ 6. Mother cats carry their babies around.

_____ 7. Baby kittens are protected by their mothers.

_____ 8. Cats are always unfriendly.

_____ 9. Mother cats pick up their kittens by their tails.

_____ 10. Cats can be playful and gentle.

REMEMBER Ask yourself questions. Read to find answers.

Spelunking

Would you like to be a spelunker? Spelunkers are people who explore caves. Just as expert spelunkers can guide you through a cave, guide words can guide you through the thousands of words in a dictionary. In this lesson, you will read about caves and spelunking. You will learn to use guide words.

1 KEYS to Guide Words

Guide words tell you what words are on a page.

LEARN Guide words are found at the top of each page in a dictionary. The guide word on the left tells you the first word on the page. The guide word on the right tells you the last word. Use alphabetical order to decide if the word you are searching for is on the page. If your word comes after the word on the left and before the word on the right, you will find it on the page.

DIRECTIONS Draw a line through any word that does not belong between the guide words in boldface type.

1. **cane**	2. **several**	3. **holiday**
camera	sew	holly
canoe	set	holster
canvas	shabby	home
cane	shot	house
cap	**shade**	**homelike**

② Practice With Guide Words

DIRECTIONS Read about caves. Then read each pair of guide words. Find three words in the box that belong on each page. Write them in alphabetical order on the lines.

cave is formed when lava from a volcano flows down a slope. A lava cave is near the earth's surface. Sea caves form on rocky shores where wind and surf wear away the rock.

spelunk	pivot	pizza
pity	tuck	sphinx
tube	speedy	Tuesday

1. pitch/placate

_____

_____

_____

A cave is a hollow area in the earth where the sun can never enter. Because of the lack of sun, the inside of a cave is dark and damp.

Most caves are formed in limestone or similar rock. Underground water slowly dissolves the rock. The water may carve out deep pits in parts of the caves. It may carve out underground lakes or rivers. Some of those rivers may even have waterfalls.

Other kinds of caves are formed in different ways. A lava

2. try/tugboat

_____

_____

_____

3. speedboat/spider

_____

_____

_____

Spelunking makes an exciting hobby, but it can be dangerous, too. Spelunkers wear tough clothing to protect themselves from dripping water and sharp rocks. They wear hardhats with headlamps. They carry a flashlight in case the headlamp fails. They also carry special ladders and ropes. Spelunkers always go into caves in groups with experienced guides.

Spelunkers often see beautiful colors in caves. Minerals in the water form colored shapes like icicles. These shapes may hang from the ceiling or rise up from the cave floor. Experienced spelunkers take special care to keep from damaging a cave. They never break off or remove the fragile rock formations. Damage to a cave can never be repaired.

Some caves are not very deep. Others are many miles in length. Many longer caves have winding passages to explore. There are passages that no human has ever seen.

Some of the most beautiful caves are open to the public. The Carlsbad Caverns are in the state of New Mexico. The longest cave system in the world is Mammoth Cave in Kentucky. There are lakes and rivers among the 190 miles of fascinating passages. In California, the Lava Beds National Monument has more than 300 caves formed by flowing lava.

Caves are truly one of nature's wonderful sights. No wonder spelunking spelunkers like to spelunk.

Here's a cave that needs exploring! Begin with the first guide word in green at the entrance to the cave. Follow the path to the next green guide word. Circle each word that belongs between the guide words. Write each word you circle on the lines at the bottom of the page.

CAVE ENTRANCE

hoof

hog

Indiana

Hooray

hurricane

yesterday

year

You

zero

zebra

lumpy

mile

male

made

make-believe   it   know

hut   kind   kettledrum

_____! _____ _____ _____!

REMEMBER Guide words help you find your way through a dictionary.

Where Is That Book?

Books in the library are easy to find if you know the secret code. In this lesson, you will learn to break the code. You will learn to find just the book you want in a hurry.

 1 ## KEYS to Finding Books

Fiction books are stories. Non-fiction books are fact.

LEARN Fiction books are made-up stories. All fiction books in the library have a code on their spines. The letter *F* or the abbreviation *Fic* appears above the first letter of the author's last name.

Fiction books are in the fiction section of the library. They are arranged in alphabetical order. Look for the first letter of the author's last name.

Non-fiction books are filled with facts. If they are stories, they are stories about things that really happened. Non-fiction books have a number code above the first letter of the author's last name.

The shelves for non-fiction books have numbers. The numbers match the numbers on the code on the book's spine.

DIRECTIONS Read the codes. Even without the title, you can tell whether a book is fiction or non-fiction. Write F for fiction or N-F for non-fiction on the line beside each spine.

_____ 1.   _____ 2.   _____ 3.

_____ 4.   _____ 5.   _____ 6.

DIRECTIONS The books on the shelves are all mixed up. Help straighten them out. Decide whether the books are fiction or non-fiction. Write their titles in the right place on the correct shelf.

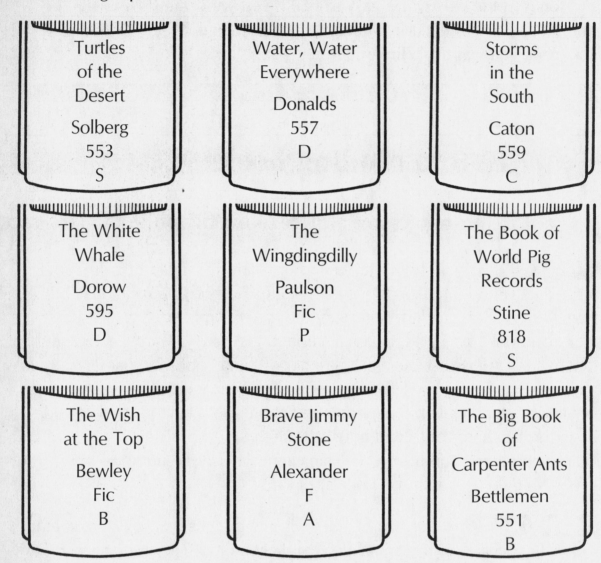

Turtles
of the
Desert

Solberg
553
S

Water, Water
Everywhere

Donalds
557
D

Storms
in the
South

Caton
559
C

The White
Whale

Dorow
595
D

The
Wingdingdilly

Paulson
Fic
P

The Book of
World Pig
Records

Stine
818
S

The Wish
at the Top

Bewley
Fic
B

Brave Jimmy
Stone

Alexander
F
A

The Big Book
of
Carpenter Ants

Bettlemen
551
B

1. Fiction

<hr />   <hr />   <hr />

2. Non-fiction

<hr />   <hr />   <hr />

<hr />   <hr />   <hr />

3 Read and Apply

DIRECTIONS Read the book reviews. Decide whether each book is fiction or non-fiction. Choose the correct code from the box. Write the code for each book on the line.

Fic	597	614
H	H	W
F	636	Fic
S	B	W

1. Clarence Hylander has written a very interesting book. *Animal in Armor* tells unusual facts about the habits of animals like turtles, snakes, and armadillos.

_____

2. *Charlotte's Web* by E. B. White tells the story of barnyard animals who are organized by a spider and a girl to save the life of a young pig.

_____

3. The zaniest kid in town is forever getting into something in the imaginary tale of *Peter Potts* by Clifford Hicks.

_____

4. Interesting studies of animal training are reported by Bruce Buchenholz in *A Way with Animals.*

_____

5. Anyone who wants to learn about good eating habits would like *Bugs in the Peanut Butter* by Michael Weiner.

_____

6. Brenda Sivers weaves a delightful story of a young boy who does what he thinks is best despite what others say in *The Snailman.*

_____

Read each statement. Circle T if the statement is true. Circle F if the statement is false.

1. Fiction books are shelved alphabetically. T F

2. Fiction books are shelved by the author's last name. T F

3. A book with the code **939**
   T is a fiction book. T F

4. A story book with a made-up story would be found in the fiction section. T F

5. A book about different breeds of dogs would be found in the non-fiction section. T F

6. Non-fiction books are shelved numerically by call number. T F

7. A book with **Fic**
   W on its spine would come before a book

   with **Fic**
   G . T F

8. A book of facts and rules about hockey would be in the fiction section. T F

9. Books with the call numbers **436**   **859**
   W and **P** are non-fiction. T F

10. Fairy tales can be found in the non-fiction section. T F

11. Books with these codes would be shelved in this order:
    Fic Fic Fic Fic
     T V R W . T F

12. Books with these codes would be shelved in this order:
    348 385 736 802
     T H P F T F

REMEMBER It's easy to find the right book when you know the code.

128 Locating Books

Looking for Books

The card catalogue is an index to the whole library. In this lesson, you will learn to use the card catalogue to find any book in the library.

 ## KEYS to Using the Card Catalogue

Alphabetical order can help you find books.

LEARN   A card catalogue is a large file with many drawers. Every book in the library is in the card catalogue. Every drawer in a card catalogue has a label. The label tells you which letters are filed in the drawer.

Every book has three cards. One card is filed by the author's last name. Another card is filed by the book's title. The third card tells the subject of the book. You can look up any book by its author, title, or subject.

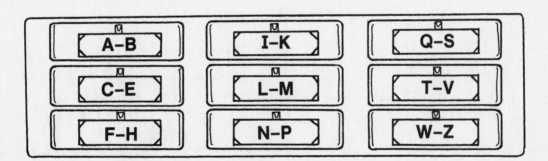

DIRECTIONS Use the card catalogue to find books on these subjects. Which drawer would you use for each subject? Write its letters on the line.

1. softball

2. hats

3. frogs

4. dogs

5. zebras

6. robots

7. music

8. vans

9. dolls

10. oceans

11. knots

12. jets

2 Practice Using the Card Catalogue

DIRECTIONS Have you ever wished a book would never end? You might like other books by the same author. The card catalogue can help. Authors are filed in the card catalogue by their last names.

Read the author's names. Write each name as it would look in the card catalogue. Circle the letter you would use. Write the letters of the correct drawer. The first one is done for you.

1. Beverly Cleary

Ⓒleary, Beverly   C–E

2. Tasha Tudor

_____

3. Leo Lionni

_____

4. Russell Hoban

_____

DIRECTIONS Maybe a friend told you about a good book. You can find it in the card catalog. Use the first word in the title of most books. If a book begins with *a, an,* or *the,* use the next word.

In each book title, circle the letter you would use to find the card. Write the letters of its file drawer on the line.

1. A Special Trick   _____

2. Jumanji   _____

3. Blueberries for Sal   _____

4. An Awesome Thing   _____

5. Pumpkin Moonshine   _____

6. The Stupids Step Out   _____

DIRECTIONS Write each book, subject, or author on a line in the correct drawer.

Eric and Matt are hospital volunteers. Their job is to get library books for the patients. First they write down the patients' requests. Then they sort out their list. When they get to the library, they each take a different drawer. Soon they have all the books they need.

1. *I'll Fix Anthony*
2. any book about horses
3. *Norman the Doorman*
4. *The Book of Giant Stories*
5. any book by Maurice Sendak
6. any book about monkeys
7. any book by Joan Tate
8. *The Half-A-Moon Inn*
9. any book about cars
10. *William's Doll*

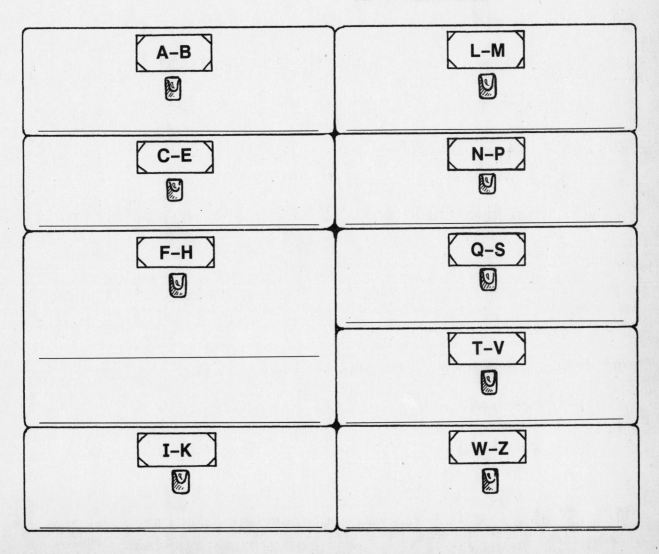

Use the card catalogue in the picture to help you answer the questions.

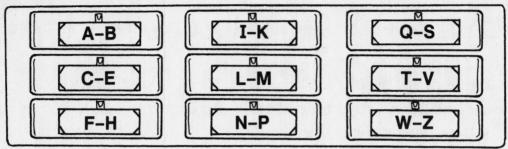

1. Name three types of cards in a card catalogue. _____

   _____ _____

2. Would you find the title or author card for Lucille Clifton's book, *The Lucky Stone,* in the L-M drawer? _____

3. In which drawer would find a card for a book about caterpillars?

   _____

4. In which two drawers would find cards for *The Magic Finger* by Roald Dahl? _____ _____

5. Which drawer has a card for *Charlotte's Web?* _____

6. Which two drawers have cards for a book of poems by Judith Viorst?

   _____ _____

7. Benjamin Appel's book, *Heart of Ice,* would have a title card in the _____ drawer.

8. Which drawers have the title and author cards for Phyllis LaFarge's book, *The Gumdrop Necklace?* _____ _____

9. Where would you look to find out about cowboys? _____

REMEMBER Find the books you want in the card catalogue

Prima Ballerina

When you want to find information in a hurry, the encyclopedia is a good place to look. In this lesson, you will learn to find information in an encyclopedia. You will read about a famous ballerina.

1 KEYS to Using the Encyclopedia

It's as easy as ABC.

LEARN Encyclopedias are reference books. You can find them in the library. Most encyclopedias have several volumes. The topics are listed in alphabetical order. People are listed by their last names.

Study the set of encyclopedias in the picture. There are twenty-one volumes. Each volume has a number. Each volume also has guide letters.

A	B	C-Ch	Ci-Cz	D	E	F	G	H	I	J-K	L	M	N-O	P	Q-R	S-Sn	So-Sz	T	U-V	WX YZ
1	2	3	4	5	6	7	8	9	10	11	12	13	14	15	16	17	18	19	20	21

DIRECTIONS Which volume would you use to find information on each topic below? Write its number on the line beside each topic. Use the encyclopedias in the picture.

_____ 1. ballet

_____ 2. Abraham Lincoln

_____ 3. theater

_____ 4. Laura Ingalls Wilder

_____ 5. Eleanor Roosevelt

_____ 6. symphonies

_____ 7. opera

_____ 8. Thomas Edison

DIRECTIONS Before you can locate a topic in the encyclopedia, you need to decide what the topic is. Suppose someone asks you, "When was the first telegraph sent?" Which word in the question is the topic? If you chose *telegraph,* you found the key topic.

Do not answer the questions below. Instead, find the key topic. Write the word you would look up on the line.

1. What was "Babe" Ruth's real name? _____

2. Who invented the helicopter? _____

3. Where do cheetahs live? _____

4. When was Susan B. Anthony born? _____

5. How was the game of baseball invented? _____

6. What country did collies come from? _____

7. How old is the oldest living redwood tree? _____

8. How is frost formed on windows? _____

9. Who is Disney World named for? _____

10. How can a mistletoe plant kill a tree? _____

11. How long have computers been used? _____

12. How many breeds of cats are there? _____

Read and Apply

Read about Suzanne Farrell, a famous ballerina.

The ballet students strained to see the bulletin board.

"Hurry, Roberta," called a friend. "The parts for *The Nutcracker* have finally been posted."

Roberta Sue Flicker didn't hurry. She knew she would get a boy's part. She always got a boy's part because she was tall. When she finally read the bulletin board, she got the surprise of her life. She would be dancing the role of Clara. She was so excited. She practiced and practiced.

When the night of the show came, Roberta had a splinter in her foot. She was in pain with every step she danced. The splinter didn't stop her, though. She danced perfectly. After the ballet, she knew she had found her life's goal. She would become a prima ballerina.

Two years later, she got her chance. She tried out for a scholarship with the New York City Ballet. She went to New York. She took more lessons. She worked hard. In 1961, she became the youngest member of the company. She took the stage name Suzanne Farrell.

That name became famous. By 1963, she was a solo dancer. Her name and picture were in all the dance magazines. In 1965, she was named the principal dancer of the New York City Ballet.

In 1969, Suzanne Farrell left the New York City Ballet. She toured Europe. People all over Europe loved her, too. She became an international star. She won many awards. In 1976, she won a very special award. It came from *Dance* magazine. This award made Roberta Flicker's dream come true. She was named "America's Prima Ballerina."

1. Roberta studied other subjects besides dance. Which volume would she have used to find information about these subjects?

_____ a. art   _____ b. music

_____ c. French   _____ d. acting

_____ **a.** cello

_____ **b.** flute

_____ **c.** drum

_____ **d.** clarinet

_____ **e.** viola

_____ **f.** cornet

_____ **g.** trombone

_____ **h.** saxophone

_____ **i.** tympani

2. An article on art would come before or after an article about acting?

_____

3. When studying music, Roberta may have needed information about musical instruments. Which volume would she have used for each instrument?

4. Underline the key topic in each question. Do not answer the question. Write the number of the volume in which you would find the topic.

   a. In what year was the first ballet performed? _____

   b. In what country was George Balanchine born? _____

Good Notes Make Good Sense

If you've ever made a list, you have already taken notes. In this lesson, you will learn rules for good notetaking. You will practice taking notes to help you at home and at school.

 ## KEYS to Notetaking

Organize. Be neat. Keep your notes in a special place.

LEARN Notes can't help you unless you can find them and read them later. Follow three rules to take useful notes.

Rule 1: Organize your notes to make them easy to use.
Rule 2: Be neat so you can read your notes later.
Rule 3: Keep your notes in a special notebook.

DIRECTIONS Marlene and Joanne each have a job. Their mothers asked them to stop at the store after school. Both Marlene and Joanne took notes. Marlene used her assignment notebook. Joanne wrote her shopping list on a scrap of paper. Look at the notes each girl took. Circle the correct answer for each question.

Marlene's Notes

O	Shopping List		
	Dairy	Bread	Canned Goods
O	milk	bread	tuna
	butter	cookies	Other
			T.V. magazine
O			

Joanne's Notes

milk
bread
butter
T.V. magazine
cookies
tuna

1. Whose notes are more organized?   Marlene   Joanne

2. Who probably finished more quickly?   Marlene   Joanne

DIRECTIONS Read the story. Read the details below it. Cross out any details you don't need to remember. Write the ones you need to remember in the notebook. Remember to fill in the date and heading.

Your science teacher has a surprise for you. You will be doing something special in class on Monday. You can only do the activity if you remember to bring in supplies. You will need a cup, some soil, and a small box. You will need one more thing, but your teacher will bring that.

If you forget your supplies, you will work on another project. You will copy a science article out of the encyclopedia.

The special activity sounds interesting. You sure don't want to copy an article out of the encyclopedia. It's a long time until Monday though. How will you remember what to bring?

Details

a cup

an encyclopedia

some soil

the teacher's surprise

your gym shoes

a small box

○		
	Date	Heading
○	1.	
	2.	
	3.	
○		

3 Read and Apply

DIRECTIONS Read each story. Decide which ideas you need to remember. Write your notes on the notebook page. Include a date and a heading.

A. On Monday, your teacher gives you some seeds. You pack soil in the cup, then push your seeds down. Finally, you cover the top with water. You pack your plant in the small box.

At the end of the day, your teacher tells you how to take care of the seed at home. He says to place the plant in a sunny spot. Check the plant every day. If the soil is dry, water it lightly.

A plant in your room would be nice. How will you remember what to do?

B. When you get home from school, no one is home but your father. He is very busy. He asks you to answer the phone.

The phone rings and rings. Your sister's boyfriend wants her to call him. Your friend Alan invites you to the circus. Your mother should call his mother if you can go. Mr. Ames calls your father and leaves his number. The number is 555-3456.

You will be in big trouble if you don't get all the messages right. What will you do?

C. Last week you missed too many words on the spelling test. Your best friend Craig got them all right. Craig tells you his special plan for studying his words.

First Craig writes the word. He spells it in a whisper as he writes it. Then he closes his eyes and pictures the way the word looks. Then he looks at it once more. After that, Craig covers the word again and writes it without looking. He checks to see if he made any mistakes. If he made mistakes, he circles them.

If Craig gets the word right, he doesn't study it again for a while. If he misses the word, he starts over.

You're willing to try anything that will help. How will you remember all those steps?

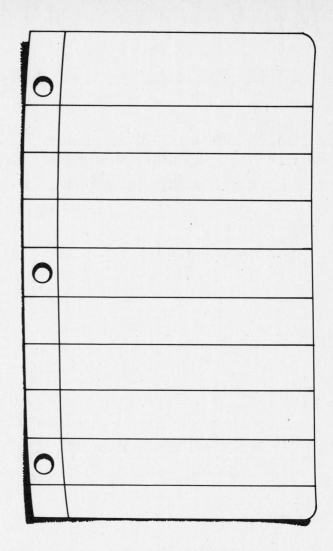

Rule 1: Organize your notes to make them easy to read.

Rule 2: Be neat so you can read your notes later.

Rule 3: Keep your notes in a special notebook.

REMEMBER Follow the rules to take notes that will help you.

Hubert Lee

Everyone is afraid of something. Do you think that statement is true or false? In this lesson, you will read about a bear who must conquer a fear. You will also learn an easy way to keep track of important facts when you read.

 KEYS to Mapping

Story maps help you find your way around a story.

LEARN A story map is a picture of what you read. The picture helps you organize important facts. It helps you remember what you have read.

DIRECTIONS Read the paragraph. The main topic is already in the middle circle. Put the subtopics in the other circles. Trace the dotted lines to connect the main idea with the other ideas.

Most people have fears at some time in their lives. To those who can't swim, water may be frightening. Some people get nervous during a thunderstorm. Looking down at the bottom of a deep canyon can be frightening for people who fear heights.

Ideas: People have fears.
Water
Storms
Height

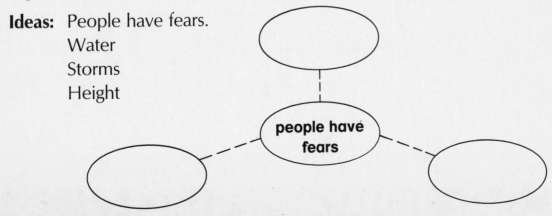

people have
fears

DIRECTIONS Read the story. Decide which idea is the main idea and which ideas are subtopics. Complete the story map.

Woodchucks, bears, and frogs all spend the whole winter sleeping. This long winter sleep is called hibernation. Animals hibernate to protect themselves from the cold. They are able to stay alive during the time of year when food is hard to find.

When a woodchuck is ready to hibernate, it curls up into a ball in its underground home. The woodchuck's sleep is different from the kind people have at night. The woodchuck's heart slows down. Its breathing almost stops.

Frogs hibernate, too. Their bodies get very cold. They seem to be dead. They are not dead, though. When spring comes and the ground and air warm up, the frog will come to life again.

Bears hibernate in caves. Their bodies do not get as cold as the bodies of smaller animals. This is because their bodies are so large.

Ideas: Hibernating
Woodchucks
Frogs
Bears

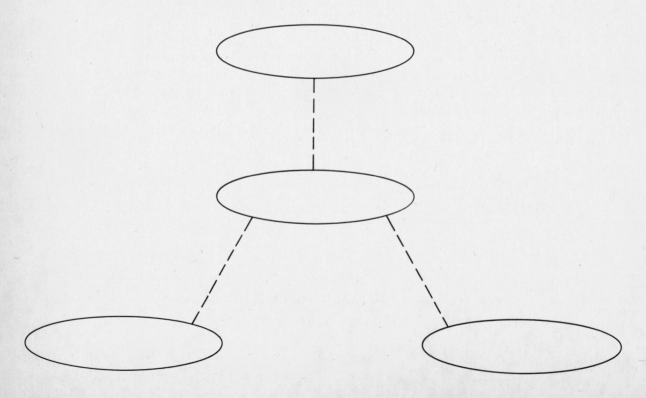

DIRECTIONS How would you map this story about a young bear?

All day Hubert worried. It was almost time to start his long winter nap. Hubert hated this time of year. He was afraid of the dark. At noon his friend Charley Chipmunk came over. He saw the worried look on Hubert's face.

"What's wrong?" Charlie asked.

Hubert Lee didn't want to admit his fear. He thought he was too old to be afraid of the dark. He needed Charley's help, though. He decided he had to tell.

"Everybody's afraid of something," said Charley. "We'll find out what the others do to get over their fears. Let's go!"

Charley and Hubert walked to Woody Woodchuck's house.

"Were you ever afraid of the dark?" Hubert asked Woody.

"Yes," said Woody. "Then I learned to close my eyes before my mother turned out the light. I never saw the dark when it came."

That night Hubert couldn't wait to go to bed. He closed his eyes while the lights were still on. After a while, his mother quietly turned them off. Hubert waited to fall

asleep. When he couldn't wait any more, he opened his eyes. He was still afraid.

Hubert did not give up. He asked Sammy Squirrel what he did when he was afraid of the dark.

"I played the radio," said Sammy. "That made me feel better. After I fell asleep, my mother came in and turned the radio off."

That night Hubert went to bed early. He turned his radio on and soon was fast asleep. When his mother turned the radio off, Hubert woke up. It was very dark and quiet. He was still afraid.

Since there was only one day left before his nap, Hubert was desperate. He asked some children what they did when they were afraid of the dark.

"We sleep with these," they all answered at once. They held up their fuzzy teddy bears.

Hubert rushed home and picked up his favorite stuffed toy. It was a toy human dressed like a football player. He crawled into his bed with his soft, cuddly toy in his arms and fell fast asleep.

Hubert slept and slept, and if it's still winter, he's probably sleeping right now.

DIRECTIONS Make your own map of this story about Hubert Lee. Put the main topic in a circle in the middle. Put the names of the people Hubert talked to in circles around the main idea. Put the solutions they offered in circles connected to each name.

REMEMBER Maps are your guides to stories.

"I have to go shopping today," said Old Ma Potts the next morning.

"Can I come?" asked Henry.

"I'm afraid not," said Old Ma Potts. "If you come in the car there won't be room for the groceries."

"I'll go for a walk then," said Henry.

"Be careful," warned Old Ma Potts. "Don't run about."

"I won't," said Henry.

"Don't try to play with other dogs!"

"I won't," said Henry.

"And whatever you do, don't go swimming! You might get your paws tangled in your ears and drown."

"I won't go swimming," said Henry.

"Good boy," said Old Ma Potts. She patted him and went away in her little blue car.

Henry sighed. Then he started down the lane, with his ears trailing behind him. When he reached the park, he sat down under a tree.

The fuzzy dog and the boy were playing with a stick.

"Want a game?" asked the dog, putting one paw on the stick.

When they had gone, Henry felt very sad. "Time to go home," said Old Ma Potts, and she picked up his ears. When they got home, Henry backed into his doghouse, and pulled his ears in after him. He put his head on his paws and went to sleep. In his dreams, he ran about. He played with other dogs. He went swimming. And his ears were small like the ears of other dogs.

"I can't," said Henry gloomily.

"Why not?" asked the fuzzy dog.

"Because of my ears," said Henry.

"Oh," said the fuzzy dog. "They are pretty big, aren't they? I suppose they must be heavy to carry about—especially when they get wet."

"They don't," said Henry.

"What? NEVER! How about if you go swimming?"

"I don't go swimming," said Henry.

"What about rain then?" asked the fuzzy dog.

"If it rains I stay at home in my doghouse," said Henry.

"FETCH!" called the boy, and threw the stick.

"Come for a run!" invited the fuzzy dog, wagging his fuzzy tail.

"I can't," said Henry.

"Oh well!" said the fuzzy dog. He ran off and the boy followed.

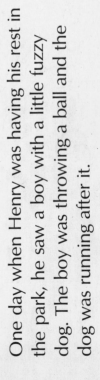

One day when Henry was having his rest in the park, he saw a boy with a little fuzzy dog. The boy was throwing a ball and the dog was running after it.

Henry sat and watched. He couldn't stand it! What was the use of being a dog if he couldn't run about like other dogs? He got up and tried to run. Thud! He had tripped over his ears.

"But I am a dog," said Henry to himself. "So I'll act like a dog!" He got up and tried again.

THUD!

Now since Henry couldn't run about or play with other dogs, or go swimming in the creek or do any of the things he wanted to do, he was very bored.

He used to walk slowly down to the end of the lane to the park. He'd sit down and have a rest, and then walk slowly home again. Old Ma Potts would go with him, to carry the ears.

"I thought you said you never got wet?" said the little fuzzy dog, bounding by with his stick.

"I don't," said Henry.

"Well you will now!" said the fuzzy dog. "It's going to rain!"

HOME SWEET HOME

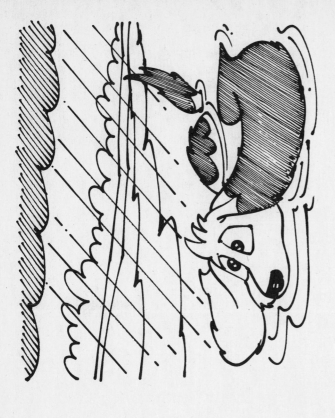

Henry scrambled up. The first raindrops were already falling. Even if he hurried he could never get home in time.

"If I'm going to get wet I might as well do it properly," said Henry and he went down to the creek. Soon his paws were wet. His sides were wet. His back was wet. And his ears were—floating! Henry swam.

Henry lived with Old Ma Potts. She tried to tie his ears up with a shoe lace. Then she used a clothes pin. She even tried a hair net!

They worked for a while, but then—down would come the ears. FLOP! One on either side of Henry's face. Henry would have to stop and sit down, because he couldn't walk without tripping over the ends of his ears.

When he was wet enough, he paddled to the bank and shook himself. He felt so dizzy that he fell over. What was the matter? Henry got up carefully and looked from one side to the other.

Where were his ears? He could just see two hairy fringed ends. He turned around twice. He sat down and shook his head. What had happened?

And by the time Henry was two—the ears were twice the size of Henry!

When Henry was six months old, the ears were half as big as he was.

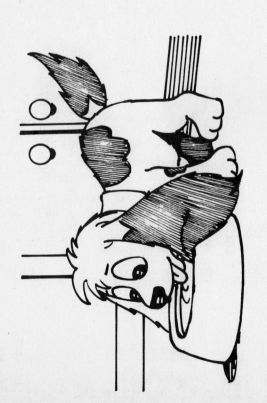

When Henry was a year old, he and the ears were the same size.

Henry bounded home through the rain, feeling as light as a wet dog could. Old Ma Potts was waiting for him on the doorstep. She was looking down the lane. At first she didn't recognize him. Then she did.

"Henry! You've been running about!"

"That's right," he said.

"Henry! You've been playing!"

"I have," said Henry.

"Henry! You've been *swimming!*"

"Yes," said Henry.

"Henry! What's happened to your ears?"

"They must have shrunk while I was in the water," said Henry.

"Now why didn't I think of trying that long ago!" said Old Ma Potts. "Well! Let's go for a walk in the rain to celebrate!"

And they did.

Henry was a dog. He would have been a very handsome dog if it hadn't been for one thing.

His ears were huge.

They were enormous!

They were gigantic!

Even when Henry was a puppy he had trouble with those ears. The ears dingle dangled. His feet were all tangled. And as Henry grew the ears did too!

Henry's Ears

by

Sally Farrell Odgers